PRAISE FOR EARLIER EDITIONS OF *HOW TO GET A JOB YOU'LL LOVE*

'John Lees is one of the grand masters in the burgeoning field of careers coaching. His practical yet inspiring approach helps people not only to make the right career decisions but to work out how they can live their lives to the full, and with meaning.'

Liz Hall, Editor, *Coaching at Work*

'No matter how many barriers – real or imagined – are currently preventing you making the career change you know you need, this book will help you demolish them more effectively than a wrecking ball. John's books are thought-provoking, stimulating, challenging and a pleasure to read – and this is no exception. It could well change your life.'

Steve Crabb, Editor, *People Management*

'It shouldn't just be another job. It should be a job that you will enjoy – you will be better in it, it will give you energy and develop your potential. We are totally behind the challenge in the title *How to Get a Job You'll Love*, so much so, that we regularly give his book to CMC clients.'

**Robin Wood, Managing Director,
Career Management Consultants Limited**

'I have a job I love but I still read this book and got lots out of it. If I ever want to change my job, this book is the first place I'd go for advice and inspiration.'

Charlotte Hindle, Freelance Writer

'This book will certainly get you thinking. Being self-aware is a skill that all great leaders possess. John Lees teaches you how to develop your own self-awareness and how to use that awareness effectively to achieve career success.'

Carol Lewis, Editor, Career, *The Times*

'John Lees provides sound, knowledgeable advice, and coaching, especially in terms of the emotional and practical impact of career and, therefore life change events. Although I had activated my personal network to good effect, and felt I was in control of my own "destiny", I found John's counsel extremely helpful in "de-stressing" the situation. Having someone of John's calibre confirm and expand on the activities I was undertaking in the pursuit of a new career opportunity, and the explanation of the usual time-scales involved, provided a positive influence to my confidence about the short- and long-term future options.'

**Kath Lowey, Head of Customer Service,
'ng HR Services**

FURTHER PRAISE FOR JOHN LEES' WORK

'John Lees is brilliant at creating the kind of mind shift we all need to see ourselves and our work in a way that lets us transform both.'
Maureen Rice, Editor, *PSYCHOLOGIES*

'John Lees inspires people to rethink the way they work: to work with greater purpose, meaning and life/work balance.'
Andrea Watson, Editor, *Daily Express* CAREERS

'You can always rely on John Lees to come up with helpful, practical advice that is both accessible and effective.'
Terry Gibson, Editor of *AMED Organisations & People*

'John Lees uses his considerable experience of the world of work to write practical and readable books that can help you move forward in your career. He's also very useful if you want great quotes for careers features.'
Adeline Iziren, regular *Guardian* contributor and founder of Smartgraduates.com

'John Lees produces books which are inspirational. They are easy to read and make sense to everyday life. His writing is challenging and thought-provoking whilst never moving out of the real world. Any John Lees book is a must if you are planning your career.'
Amanda Green, Careers Coach and Reviewer for *Career Guidance Today Magazine*

'Highly recommended – always practical, but never patronising.'
Ian Wylie, Editor of *Guardian Rise*

'John Lees writes in a clear thinking style about practical ways to manage a career journey in competitive times.'
Mark Venning, President, Association of Career Professionals International

'Excellent advice to help you take charge of your career and manage it positively.'
Jo Bond, Managing Director, Right Coutts

'Career advice with a difference, John Lees delivers a clear and comprehensive step-by-step guide to making your dream job a reality.'
Sam Dukes, Editor, *EDGE* (Institute of Leadership & Management)

'I love John's straight-up approach. There's nothing airy-fairy about the career advice in his books and yet the tone holds your interest, not the usual dry-as-a-bone business book banter. What I love most is that it's real-life, real-world stuff: first he guides you to making your own career decisions with passion and instinct but then he gives professional, realistic – and very grown up – advice about making those decisions happen. I can still remember reading *How to Get a Job You'll Love* as a young journalist fresh off the boat from Oz with zilch industry contacts. Now I am in my dream job – John's advice works, pure and simple.'

Anna Magee, Health Editor, *RED*

'John Lees' advice is witty, incisive and really works – a real breath of fresh air for those who want to change the course of their working lives.'

Tessa Williams, Journalist and Contributor of *EVE Magazine*

How to Get a Job You'll Love

A practical guide to unlocking your talents and finding your ideal career

2009–10 Edition

John Lees

The McGraw·Hill Companies

London • Burr Ridge IL • New York • St Louis • San Francisco • Auckland
Bogotá • Caracas • Lisbon • Madrid • Mexico • Milan
Montreal • New Delhi • Panama • Paris • San Juan • São Paulo
Singapore • Sydney • Tokyo • Toronto

How to Get a Job You'll Love:
A practical guide to unlocking your talents and finding your ideal career
2009–10 Edition
John Lees

ISBN-10: 007712180-5
ISBN-13: 978-007712180-8

 **Professional**

Published by McGraw-Hill Professional
Shoppenhangers Road
Maidenhead
Berkshire
SL6 2QL
Telephone: 44 (0) 1628 502 500
Fax: 44 (0) 1628 770 224
Website: www.mcgraw-hill.co.uk

British Library Cataloguing in Publication Data
A catalogue record for this book is available from the British Library

Library of Congress Cataloguing in Publication Data
The Library of Congress data for this book
is available from the Library of Congress

Typeset by Gray Publishing, Tunbridge Wells, Kent
Cover design by Two Associates
Printed and bound in Finland by WS Bookwell

McGraw-Hill books are available at special quantity discounts.
Please contact the Corporate Sales Executive

*The **McGraw·Hill** Companies*

About the Author

John Lees is one of the UK's best-known career coaches. *How To Get A Job You'll Love* regularly tops the list as the best-selling careers book by a British author, and along with *Job Interviews: Top Answers To Tough Questions* has been selected as WH Smith's 'Business Book of the Month'.

As a career-transition coach, John specializes in helping people make difficult career decisions: either difficult because they don't know what to do next, or because there are barriers in the way of success. He regularly delivers events for both career-changers and practitioners across the UK and has also undertaken workshops in the USA and South Africa. He is a regular keynote speaker at UK events (including *One Life Live* and *Forum 3*) and has featured as a speaker at the world's largest international career conferences in the USA.

John writes regularly for *The Times*, *The Guardian*, *Personnel Today* and *People Management*, and his work has been featured on TV (he was a presenter on the BBC interactive 'Back to Work' programme), extensively on radio, and in many publications including *Management Today*, *Cosmopolitan*, *Daily Express*, *Daily Mirror*, *Real World*, *Financial World*, *Pathfinder*, *Psychologies*, *Eve* and *She*. His work and case studies have been profiled in *Coaching at Work* and *The Sunday Times*.

John is a graduate of the universities of Cambridge, London and Liverpool, and has spent most of his career focusing on the world of work. He has trained recruitment specialists since the mid-1980s, and is the former Chief Executive of the Institute of Employment Consultants (now the REC). He now runs his own careers consultancy and is also retained as a Senior Associate by outplacement specialists Career Management Consultants Ltd. He has been elected as a Career Management Fellow (CMF) by the Institute of Career Certification International.

As an ordained Anglican priest John works as volunteer clergy in the Diocese of Chester, and has a particular interest in vocations and the spiritual dimension of work. He lives and works in Cheshire, with his wife, the children's writer, Jan Dean, with occasional visits from their two adult sons.

John Lees Associates provides one-to-one career coaching in most parts of the UK. For details plus information about talks and workshops given by John Lees visit the website www.johnleescareers.com or telephone 01565 631625.

Other careers books by John Lees published by McGraw-Hill Professional
See www.jobyoulove.co.uk

Job Interviews: Top Answers To Tough Questions **(2008), £9.99, ISBN 9780077119096**
Lists over 200 interview questions typically asked by employers and recruiters including the kind that will throw you completely unless you have prepared carefully. Also a range of tips about multi-strategy job search and using your CV in the interview process.

Take Control of Your Career **(2006), £12.99, ISBN 9780077109677**
How to manage your manager once you've got a job, learning how to read your organization, avoid career traps, renegotiate your job role and enhance your career without losing control of your life balance.

Why You? – CV Messages To Win Jobs **(2007), £9.99, ISBN 9780077115104**
Building on an extensive review of what employers love and hate about CVs, helps you decide which CV format will work best for you and reveals the secrets of a strong, effective document that gets you short listed.

ACKNOWLEDGEMENTS

This book is written standing on the shoulders of two career coaching giants: Dick Bolles and Daniel Porot.

My gratitude goes to all those who have prompted ideas or encouraged various editions: Judith Armatage, Liz Baldwin, Jane Bartlett, Gill Best, Simon Chesters, Claire Coldwell, John Courtis, Liz Cross, Margaret Dale, John Eardley, Ron Feasey, Liz Hall, Peter Hawkins, Deirdre Hughes, Gayle Lantz, Mary Maybin, Brian McIvor, Bernard Pearce, Carole Pemberton, Stuart McIntosh, Stuart Mitchell, Andrew O'Hanlon, Amiel Osmaston, Stuart Robertson, Ray Samuels, Lorraine Silverman, Peter Sinclair, Philip Spencer, Ian Webb, Janie Wilson. Special thanks go to Robin Wood, MD of Career Management Consultants Limited, for giving me the opportunity to road-test many of these ideas.

Particular thanks to my brother, Andrew Lees, for great insights into the way scientists think. I am indebted to Stephanie Clarke for her website research, and to Sue Blake, who is quite possibly the best publicist on the planet.

My immense gratitude goes to all the McGraw-Hill team for steering this fifth edition into print, particularly Derek Stordahl, Katherine Wood and Sally Ashworth, and to my editors Elizabeth Choules and Julia Scott for their patient expertise.

This book is dedicated to my wife, Jan, for giving me space to find out.

Contents

Preface

WORK – YOUR FUTURE

Most people spend more time planning a car purchase, one annual holiday or their new kitchen than they do thinking about their career. Generally speaking, we're not good at career planning at all. It's staggering how many people drift from one job to another with no clear idea of the way their career is heading.

It's easy to think of career management as a crisis activity. *I must get out of here. I must find work. I've got to get a better job.* You do need to plan your career at times of transition: when you leave full-time education, when you are out of work or underemployed, or when you have a strong impulse to move on and make progress. Sometimes a sense of career crisis is expressed as an overwhelming need to do something more meaningful or relevant.

WHO IS THIS BOOK FOR?

This book is written for anyone who is trying to make conscious, informed decisions about career choice. All kinds of people have difficult career decisions to make.

This book can help you if you are:

▮ leaving full-time education or seeking work after bringing up a family

▮ feeling 'stuck' and looking for new challenges, and wondering 'what on earth can I do?'

▮ ready to plan the next stage of your career

▮ facing redundancy and asking 'what do I do next?'

- ▌ unemployed and looking for better ways of identifying opportunities
- ▌ seeking work and short of ideas about job possibilities
- ▌ discouraged because you believe you have little to offer the labour market
- ▌ toying with the idea of making a complete career change

New in this edition

As well as the features which have appeared in previous editions, this edition contains new material focusing on a number of key areas.

Chapter 3, Where Next After Finishing Your Studies?, not only contains new tips for those who have taken a break to acquire qualifications, including MBA students, but also gives broad guidance to those who are leaving school or college.

There is also a great deal of new information in Chapter 10, Do You Need a Complete Change of Career?, which tries to answer the question put by many readers: 'I want to do something completely different – how do I recognize what it is?' Chapters 9 and 10 help you identify the right role, organizations and sector if you want to make a complete career change.

Appendix 2, People Who Have Transformed Their Careers, contains a range of new case studies relating the experiences of actual career changers. Appendix 3 contains an up-to-date **list of useful websites** providing career assessments, online testing and thousands of vacancies, resources to help you to find and research employers, and a wealth of organizations and their recommended websites to help you move forward.

HOW TO USE THIS BOOK

There are many 'how to' books about career change and job search. They are good at getting you organized and giving you good advice on job search.

This book aims to do something different. Its approach is to look at the way that people generate brilliant ideas and new ways of solving problems or designing products, and it then applies that breakthrough thinking to you and your career, the way you work and the way you find work. It challenges your perceived limitations and helps you to discover your strengths. Finally, it provides practical advice about making your chosen future happen.

Quite simply, the aim is to help you to make connections between your natural creativity and the way you plan your life's work.

Begin by **Working Smarter at Your Career** in Chapter 1 – take a sideways look at the way you think about yourself and the work you do. Then take a fresh look in Chapter 2 at your **career problems** – what's preventing you from getting a job you'll love?

Chapter 3 is written specially for those who will shortly be graduating or leaving full-time education: **Where Next After Finishing Your Studies?**

Before we move into the central section on working out your ideal career, Chapter 4 invites you to begin using creative strategies to revive your career by **Thinking Around Corners**. Then Chapters 5–8 offer you a step-by-step guide towards a deeper understanding of your career drivers, your chosen areas of **knowledge**, your preferred and hidden **skills**, and the key aspects of **personality** that will shape your career.

Next, some highly practical aids to achieving your goals – Chapter 11 offers a comprehensive range of **Creative Job**

Search Strategies, and Chapter 12 a guide to **Interviews and How to Survive Them**.

You'll find some unique tools to help you along your way, including the pivotal Chapter 10, **Do You Need a Complete Change of Career?**, the **House of Knowledge** (Chapter 6) – an innovative exercise to capture the things you have chosen to know about, the **Field Generator** – a ground-breaking tool to generate potential fields of work (in Chapter 9), plus a range of supporting exercises including **skill clips** (Chapter 7) and **time balance** (Chapter 13).

Career development is about much more than job search, so in Chapter 13 you will find help to **love the job you've got** – tips for renegotiating your present or future job from within, and making the best of your future career. Chapter 14 explores how you might look at a **portfolio career** now or at some stage in the future, and also explores the possibility of a **career break**.

Chapter 15 is the first step in putting things into practice, advising you how to **find a careers consultant**. Chapter 16, **Beginning it Here** ... is a five-point plan to begin to transform your career.

The book closes with a series of highly **practical checklists** covering everything from CV design to online job applications.

Does the approach work? Appendix 2 looks at people who have used the book to help them make significant career changes.

HOW THIS BOOK WILL HELP

In these pages you will look at the way businesses and individuals generate ideas about products, services and organizations, and apply that creative energy to career planning.

This book aims to unlock your hidden potential and apply it to your career and life planning, to make the way you spend your waking hours more creative, more meaningful, more enjoyable. Its focus is not on job change for its own sake. As a result of reading it, you may discover tools to improve your present job and create career opportunities where you are now.

The chapters ahead approach one major issue: your career. You may find the one tool that unlocks your potential, or you may gain multiple insights from using several ideas or exercises. One word of advice: if the exercise doesn't work for you, don't feel you have 'failed'. All it means is this: *the exercise doesn't work for you*. Put it aside and move on.

Working Smarter at Your Career

This chapter helps you to:

▮ Understand the importance of planning your career

▮ Explore the way you have made career decisions in the past

▮ Manage 'career blocks'

▮ Invent strategies for coping with personal change

▮ Handle the dark side: deal with the negatives

WHAT IS CAREER MANAGEMENT?

You probably live a life under pressure. You have to juggle priorities and manage your time. Now and again you promise yourself time out to review where you are going, but for most of us change happens when it's forced upon us.

In my work as a careers consultant I say that I specialize in helping people to make difficult career change decisions. The decisions are difficult for a variety of reasons: people don't know what they want to do next, they can't see a way out of where they are now, or they know where they want to be but don't know how to get there.

If you manage your career, actively and consciously, you will make it work better for you. Sometimes this means having a career plan over, say, 5 or 10 years. However, for others, planning ahead is far less important than being *awake* now – awake to the possibilities of change and the urgency of doing work which is more fulfilling and interesting. Those who make conscious decisions about their working lives are more successful and more satisfied. They have thought about the work they want to do and are actively pursuing it. The process has also helped them to understand what kinds of activities outside work are more rewarding. Some have sought out the right job. Others have learned the skill of redesigning the jobs that they do, so that they play to their strengths. You may recognize that your work can be adapted around you so that it is more closely related to your interests or the skills you really enjoy using. Career development doesn't always mean changing jobs.

Career management has many dimensions, including:

- discovering the kind of work you find most stimulating and enjoyable

- discovering fields of work (including jobs you didn't know existed) where you can make a difference

- striking a balance between what you are looking for and what the world has to offer – setting out the steps on your journey

- setting goals – these may be financial, learning or personal goals

- achieving the right life/work balance – making room for learning, family, relationships, and the things that matter most

- making sure that work provides the things that motivate you most – status, recognition, independence, learning, etc.

- renegotiating your job so that you can do more of the things that energize you

- planning for retirement or changes of lifestyle.

It's worth emphasizing again: if you're looking for boxes to tick, 'to do' checklists, model CVs or letters, look at one of the hundreds of books available that will give you an organized, left-brain solution. We all need good advice when it comes to managing your job search. However, this kind of book works well if you have a clear sense of direction, and all you need is a more effective job search technique. They don't help with the questions many clients express to me: 'Where the **** is my life going?' 'What on earth can I do next?' and perhaps most significantly: 'How do I make the change?'

IS WORK THAT IMPORTANT?

Judging by the amount of time spent complaining about it, it must be. A huge amount of negative energy goes into, and comes out of, work. If it wasn't for work, we would have far less to complain about.

Far too many adults of working age in Europe are either unemployed or underemployed, even in boom times. Being underemployed is as worrying as unemployment: people who are underemployed or in the wrong kind of work become demotivated, depressed or even ill. Work matters.

If we begin with life and work, we should ask ourselves one question: do you **work to live** or **live to work**?

One reason you might **work to live** is that your life's centre is outside your work. You are more motivated by the things you do outside work than the things which earn you a living. You are living out your dream in a different reality, and your salary is there simply to fund your dream. A lot of people live that way, and can be happy. Others feel that something vital is missing, but they struggle to define it.

If you work full-time hours you spend more of your life in work than in any other waking activity (if you live for 70 years, you'll spend about 23 of those years asleep, and 16 years working). Perhaps one reason you're reading this book is because you want more out of that huge slice of life we call *work*.

If you feel that you **live to work**, it may be that you've found the best job in the world. There are dangers here, too: your work/life balance may need adjustment. Perhaps work plays too important a part in your life? Those who suffer the greatest impact of redundancy are those who have made their work the most important thing in their life, perhaps at the expense of family or personal development.

WHAT IS A CAREER?

The idea that we have any choice at all in our careers is a fairly new one. Our great-grandparents' generation believed strongly in the value of hard work, in working your way up to the top, and in the idea of increasing your chances by getting a good education. It's only really since the 1950s that the Western world has grown used to the idea that we make career choices relating to our interests, personality types and backgrounds.

What is a career? To have a 'career' is largely an idea of the twentieth century. Before that, a 'job' was what we would now call an 'assignment' or 'project'; a short-term engagement. People had trades, and were 'jobbing' carpenters, masons, journalists or sailors. A permanent job was one that was attached to an income source arising from an endowment, e.g. a 'living' in a parish church or a royal appointment.

Careers are once again becoming more loose-knit and flexible. Chapter 14 offers you insights into the way you can build a portfolio career.

One definition of the word 'career' is *movement in an uncontrolled direction*, as in 'the steering failed and my car careered across the motorway'. Rapid movement in an uncontrolled direction. Does that sound familiar?

29,000 days

In the past decade the idea of career choice has become closely tied to the idea of *life choices*. In an average lifetime, a woman will live for about 29,000 days (men get rather less, about

27,600 days). That's 27,000–29,000 days to learn, work, play, raise a family, leave your mark on life or acquire wisdom. It doesn't sound a lot, does it? Certainly not a lot of days to be saying 'This isn't what I wanted to do when I grew up ...'. How you spend those days matters – no matter what your spiritual perspective.

WHAT IS CREATIVE CAREER MANAGEMENT?

Valuing creativity

The first thing to recognize is that we are all capable of inventing extraordinary solutions to cope with life's problems. For most of us these problems are everyday: taking children in opposite directions in one car, paying this week's bills with next week's money, or mending using old bits and pieces rather than buying an expensive component. Sometimes it's the kind of thinking we take for granted, such as taking an engine apart and putting it back together, perfectly, without a diagram, or caring for three or four difficult children at their most unpleasant, or making dinner out of six things found in the cupboard. We are all creative. We have to be: that's how humans have survived.

You will probably have come across many different ways of describing the way people think. However, for many of us lists, plans, diagrams and flowcharts don't work. We don't read life that way. We're inspired by conversations, by people, by movies; our natural creativity needs a different kind of kick-start.

The important thing to remember at this stage is this: we are all given a particular kind of creativity. Career choice is about unlocking what makes *you* a creative, energized person.

There is no point in work unless it absorbs you like an absorbing game.

D.H. Lawrence

What has creativity got to do with career exploration?

We normally use our creative brain to solve problems where ordinary solutions don't work. Isn't your career this kind of problem? You've tried to deal with it logically, by progressing in a sequence from A to Z. You've done the right courses, taken the right initial steps, gained the experience .... Does work provide the right answers? You've tried to look at career change as a business discipline, because you've been told that getting a job *is* a job. Maybe that worked, but did it get you the right job?

We need another method. Every day, business executives wake up and have to think of new ideas: new names for brands, new ways of selling old products, new ways of communicating with people. They have to **generate ideas** on a daily basis. Ideas come from hard work, from experience, but principally from the creative imagination. We all have it. It's the ability to think yourself into someone else's shoes, to think of possibilities, alternative futures, what ifs ....

Where do ideas come from? The age-old question of the tired mind. Writers, designers, inventors and advertising executives all have the same dread: the blank piece of paper. Yet there are ways of learning how to generate ideas. We normally look for the 'right' solution, but creativity works better where we seek multiple solutions: first one idea, then another, then another. Creativity thrives on abundance.

The vital thing is not to confuse idea generating with decision making. How many meetings have you been to where the first good idea is shot down in flames? Ideas are tentative, fragile things that in their early stages can't stand up to the strong light of decision making. It's no use thinking 'I wonder about medicine ...' if you immediately say 'Do I want to be a doctor, or don't I?' Forcing a decision too early simply crushes creative thinking. Maybe not a doctor – maybe a medical journalist, or a pharmacist, or a physiotherapist ....

When we think about ideas about our future, we must allow ideas to turn into possibilities, to allow life to be open-ended. That's where this book is designed to help.

When a business enterprise is in decline and heading towards oblivion because it has nothing interesting to offer the market-place, it needs to find a new way of thinking. Right now this business needs some smart thinking: how can it reinvent itself and turn things around? At times like this businesses throw out the rule book and become hungry for ideas that will generate new products and services. If your career is in the doldrums you may benefit from the same kind of thinking: you need to reinvent yourself, rediscover what you are capable of doing and being. As the saying goes, 'if you only live half your life, the other half will haunt you forever'.

Why do people avoid having great jobs?

There are more new jobs out there than ever before, yet at the same time we let our careers be shaped by accident, or accept second or third best because it's easier to stand still than to move forward. Most importantly of all, we insist on using the most limited kind of straight-line thinking in career planning and job search. Why? Essentially, we like to do what feels safe, even if that means being unhappy. There's a powerful part of the brain that says *stop here. It's dull, but it's comfortable. Out there looks difficult and strange.*

And then you find evidence to support your position. You focus on stories of people of your age and background who tried to make a change and failed. I have a theory. At times when change threatens we develop a personal radar that scans the horizon for information. Radar, as you know, is hungry for enemy objects. And we find them. You suddenly discover people who were made redundant and never found a job again. People beat a path to your door to tell you *don't do it … it will all come to tears.*

As you'll discover from reading this book, we come up with all kinds of negative messages to act as blocks to growth and change. If you believe 'I'm not an ideas person' or 'I'm not a leader', your brain is capable of making sure this is a self-fulfilling prophecy. If a golfer says, 'I bet I slice this ball', he probably will.

Adaptability

One of the other reasons that we avoid doing the kind of job we'd love to do is that we are adaptable. Human beings have evolved to become highly adaptable creatures, capable of living in temperatures from –30 to +50°C, and capable of living in the most demanding, unhealthy and difficult conditions. Perhaps because of this in-built survival instinct, some of us have the capacity to do something which modern society finds odd and most of history saw as the norm: to do an unpleasant job for years, or even decades. However, given a world of choice, the fact that we can carry on doing the same old job doesn't mean that we should.

Let's be realistic ...

Applied early in the process of rediscovering your potential, so-called 'realistic' thinking can be deadly, because it's all too often not about what is real but what is acceptable, conventional or safe. How many successful brands or products started life by being conventional? It is true that organizations and people all have constraints: bills to pay, mouths to feed. It's important not to underemphasize that fact. However, what matters is that these basic requirements are seen for what they area, not the centre of life.

Put another way, incremental thinking only gets you incremental results. But if you don't take even the small steps, you can pretty much guarantee that nothing will change at all.

'I just need a job'

By now you may have come to the conclusion that creative career management might be a good thing for somebody else. Why not you? Because you feel that reality is harder and tougher than that. You need something real, right now, that pays the bills. You just need a job. This might be because you're unemployed, or because you're just not paid enough to make ends meet. This places you in a vulnerable position in the labour market. It forces you to become a job beggar, going round with your hat in your hand saying just one thing: I need a job. Desperately.

I spent some time in early 2000 working with a group of job seekers from one of the townships in Johannesburg. One of them, Gugu, was aged 17 and had given up looking for work. Why? 'There are no jobs in South Africa', she said. But new jobs are being created in that country every day ... 'Yes, but so many people are chasing them', she said sadly. Talking to her I realized that too many job seekers are giving a totally undifferentiated signal. Fortunately, she and her fellow job seekers all found jobs as a result of a programme which allowed her to focus on her strengths, and gave her the tools to demonstrate them to employers.

No, it's true: I just need a job

Do you really? How long will it be before you're back asking the same questions: What am I doing this for? Where's my life going?

If that's the reality facing you, then don't use it as a justification for suppressing what you have to offer, otherwise you end up saying that there's no point thinking about my career, my skills, my future, because there are no choices. There are very few occasions when that's true. And if you need money, just earn it. Don't pretend that's all there is. We all have choices.

There will always be those who say *get real* – few of us have the luxury of career choice'. Yet we all know people who broke out of that box. Listen to successful people talking about the work they do. They don't often say 'Well, the money's good'. They talk about work being like a 'game', being 'fun' or 'the best job in the world'; they talk about the privilege of doing for a living what they would gladly do for nothing.

Another interesting fact: people get brilliant jobs even in the depths of recession. For more than a decade the UK has enjoyed low unemployment, and more people have been employed than at any time in its history, yet people still said 'this is a really bad time to be unemployed'.

How many excuses do you need to have to ensure you stay miserable at work?

Effective career planning is about finding a job that works for you, matching who you are to the life you are going to lead. That's not a luxury: that's the clearest reality there is. Doing that provides you with a great career, and gives you a greater chance of contributing to life.

Working smarter rather than harder at career building

It's sometimes said that the right job is out there somewhere looking for you, but you can't sit at home and wait for it to knock on the door. The majority of us have to rely on a mix of good judgement, inspired guesswork and a pinch of luck. Luck has been described as two mathematical laws working together: chance and averaging. We can't control chance, but we can increase the odds in our favour. Invest in your future. Use your precious thinking time carefully, and learn to think openly, because a moment's inspiration can sometimes take you far, far further than a year's dull planning.

Setting objectives is a vital part of the process. Ideas without activity are daydreams. The danger is that we move too quickly

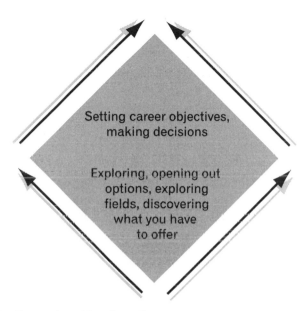

Figure 1.1 Career transition funnels

to activity without really taking the opportunity to reinvent our career. Exploring is an opening-out process. We tend to think along tramlines, moving logically from one stage to the next. Divergent thinking works rather differently. Let your imagination fan out: rather than making decisions too soon, look at possibilities. Try on ideas. Figure 1.1 shows how once you have really worked through the process of idea building, you will reach a point where you have enough information to start setting concrete objectives. At this point the funnel reverses, and you consciously close down options and aim for specific outcomes. This book takes you from the point of exploring to the point of setting real goals.

TAKE A SIDEWAYS LOOK AT CHANGE

People differ in their attitude to change. Some enjoy the energy and challenge of change, but they are often attracted by the next big new idea. Others find change disturbing because it involves moving from the known to the unknown.

Modern society seems to favour those who enjoy the excitement that comes with change. One of the difficulties of this type of person is that they sometimes make a decision based on the most radical or innovative outcome, rather than the best outcome. These **change masters** are often insensitive to the impact of change on others who are less gung-ho about the whole process.

Many people in work **suffer** change. If you feel like this, all you will hear every day is the message that 'the only certainty is the certainty of change'. I hear from fellow careers counsellors of many who feel victimized by the new culture. In a world of 'hot desking' they feel constantly anxious, unsettled – these people would work more productively if they were allowed office space to call their own. Others are fairly responsive to change if they are sold the benefits, but very wary of 'change for change's sake'.

Be experimental

To think 'it's all experimental' is a great approach to life, far better than a blame culture. Experiment and failure, 'making mistakes', is a necessary part of creative thinking. And if you are going to use the word failure, then 'fail forwards' rather than 'fail backwards'; in other words, make your mistakes positive steps forward in your learning. Every successful product brought to market required a thousand near-misses. Experiment away.

No-one can persuade another to change. Each of us guards a gate of change that can only be opened from the inside. We cannot open the gate of another, either by argument or by emotional appeal.
                                                                Marilyn Ferguson

EXERCISE 1.1 – LIFE FLOW

Draw a flowchart of your life so far, indicating all the most important steps and decisions. It might look a little like Figure 1.2.

Now look at each step in your life flow, and at each critical point draw in as many choices as you can, real, remembered or imagined, as in Figure 1.3.

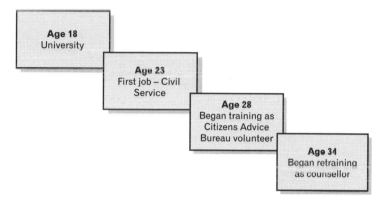

Figure 1.2   Life flow

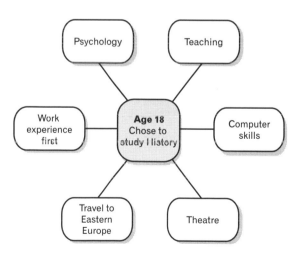

Figure 1.3   Possible choices at each turning point

EXERCISE 1.2 – MINDMAPPING YOUR FUTURE

You might find it helpful to use a **mindmap**. This is a technique pioneered by Tony Buzan which provides a tool for individual brainstorming. Place a topic at the centre of a large,

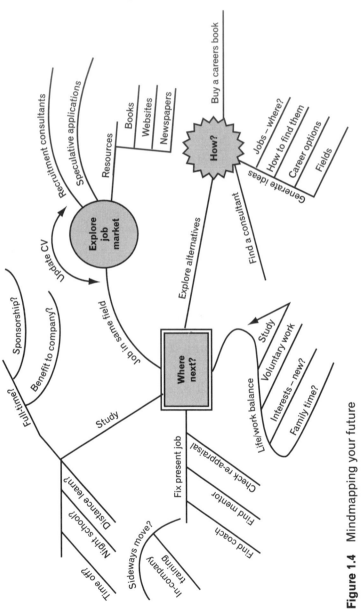

Figure 1.4 Mindmapping your future

blank piece of paper, and draw a line out of it to record a new idea. Start a new line, like the branch of a tree, to represent each new idea or connection as it comes up. Figure 1.4 shows a completed example.

EXERCISE 1.3 – FORCE FIELD ANALYSIS

This technique, devised by Kurt Lewin, presents a variation on traditional problem-solving techniques.

Draw up two columns. In column one list all the benefits that would be obtained if you manage to change your career, either by changing your job or renegotiating it. In column two list the negative forces, i.e. the forces against change. Figure 1.5 shows some typical examples.

Lewin argues that change is brought about when the driving force for change exerts greater pressure than the restraining forces that resist it. Driving forces are generally positive, reasonable and logical. In contrast, restraining forces are often negative, emotional, illogical or even unconscious. Both sets of forces are very real and must be taken seriously when dealing with any change.

Increasing the driving forces may bring results in the short term. As long as the restraining forces are still there, change becomes increasingly difficult. Think of it like pushing against a spring: at first it's easy, but the harder you push, the greater the resistance. Negative elements

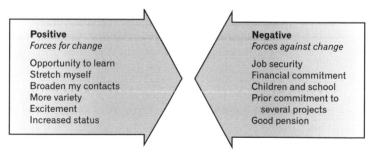

Figure 1.5   Force Field Analysis and career change

have a strong conservative factor. For example, it is often easier to stay where you are rather than face a set of difficult decisions. The fact that people dislike change is demonstrated by the fact that in the UK people change spouses more willingly than they move bank accounts, despite the huge growth in competition in the banking sector.

Using Force Field Analysis to manage personal change

▌ Draw up your own list of positive and negative factors.

▌ Add as many new positive factors as you can.

▌ Next look in detail at your negative forces. How real are they?

▌ Give each factor a score from 1 (weak) to 5 (strong).

▌ Add up the total score on each side: which side is stronger at the moment?

▌ Now we are going to make the Force Field Analysis really work. See if you can strengthen any of your positive forces. If 'opportunity to learn' is a positive factor encouraging change, then ask yourself what your job will be like if this is taken away from you. This might mean that you increase the score for factors which you discover are really important.

▌ Can you add any new positive factors? They will only make a difference if they are both real and important.

▌ Can you reduce the negative forces in any way? This means really looking at them and seeing whether you can weaken their impact or turn them into positives. How transferable is your pension? Is your present job really as secure as it seems? If you are worried about the effect of change on your family, what would be the effect if you do nothing and remain unfulfilled? If you are worried about the risk of making mistakes in a new job, then look back at your work history and think of a time when you were worried about exactly the same thing: maybe as a result you achieved something which is now a central plank of your CV?

'MUST DO' LIST

☑ Reflect: have your career decisions been made consciously, or have you largely responded to opportunity and chance?

☑ Think about how you can use this book to help. Begin a hard-back notebook to jot down your discoveries and the results of the exercises in this book. *Write down your goals*. It makes a difference.

☑ Plan ahead. Look at the chapter headings and decide how and when you are going to set aside time to go through this process.

☑ Use the Force Field Analysis technique to help someone else with personal change, and then come back to try it again for yourself.

☑ Identify someone you know who is a champion of change. Find out how and why they do it, what motivates them, and how they generate the energy to convince others.

What's the Problem?

This chapter looks at the following:

▮ The reason careers go off-line

▮ Why people follow careers they hate, and fail to get careers they would love

▮ The blocks between you and a great career

▮ Overcoming personal barriers

I DON'T HAVE TIME FOR A CAREER CRISIS ...

How many times have you heard someone talking about where they have 'ended up'? The truth is that most people are very passive about their career choices and leave job satisfaction very much to chance. It's easy to shrug off responsibility with a phrase like 'A job's a job. It pays the bills'. According to the statistical evidence, we are changing jobs ever more frequently, and because of the flexibility of the new labour market, new occupations are opening up all the time. Does this mean that people are happier in work? Does this mean that we're getting better at choosing career paths? No. According to the American writer Studs Terkel, work is, for some, 'a Monday to Friday sort of dying'.

Awareness of your work/life balance

British workers work longer hours than their counterparts in other Western European countries, but with little measurable increase in productivity. It's a culture that can be immensely damaging. In 2000 a British government report found that 80% of workplaces have employees who work more than their standard hours, and 39% without extra pay.

Why should people be happy at work?

Have you ever worked at the kind of place where they tell you 'you're not here to enjoy yourself'? What tends to happen if you believe this is that you create a world of compartments. *This is the compartment where I work. This is my family compartment. This small compartment in the corner is where I really enjoy myself.* It's all part of that either/or thinking we're so good at. I have *either* a job that pays the bills, *or* a job that's fun. I can't have both.

Carole Pemberton of Career Matters, author of several careers books, talks about the Faustian pact we make in our careers – a deal you make that allows you to think in these either/or terms, like Faust's pact with the devil. A pact typically says 'I can only be successful if …'. Here are some examples: 'I can only be a top salesperson if I work long hours and eat badly.' 'I can only be a great manager if I don't empathize with my staff.'

Why should people be happy at work? Work isn't fun, your friends will tell you. Work is real. If this all sounds reasonable, look at the people who seem to have most fun in their jobs. They're often running their own businesses, making new things, meeting new people, sharing what they know and inspiring people. Sometimes they are in jobs which directly improve the life of others. For some, it's about producing brilliant ideas, products, or great experiences for customers. Are these workers poor as a result? Sometimes. However, some of them are richer and more successful than most. Happiness and success don't always come hand in hand, but on the other hand being unhappy is no automatic route to success either. Unfortunately it's often the unhappy, unenthusiastic, low-energy people that companies get rid of first.

Why should people be happy at work? Take a deep breath. Read that question again. Work is where you spend most of your waking life. It's where you put about 80% of your personal energy. So that question really means why should people be happy? What do you think? Do happy people live longer, have great children and make a difference? You know they do. So let's stop that all-time Faustian deal: 'I can only get a great job if I forget about being happy at work.' That's a self-fulfilling deal. Be careful what you ask for in life, you might just get it … .

One of the symptoms of an approaching nervous breakdown is the belief that one's work is terribly important.

Bertrand Russell

In fact, the situation is getting worse for most of us. Research by the Work Foundation suggests that over the past decade workers in the UK have become less satisfied with their work and less productive. We're becoming increasingly dissatisfied with our jobs. We don't know whether this is because we expect more from our careers, or whether it's a national reaction to a decade of downsizing and job uncertainty. We are more prone to 'burn out', more in need of stress counselling as a result of work. It matters more than ever that we have a toolkit to help us to find a job we enjoy.

Happiness – goal or accident?

It's worth saying a little more about happiness. Many of us think that happiness is a vague, subjective and entirely individual state of mind. Others believe that we can do very little to influence or adjust happiness.

Richard Layard's book *Happiness* is one of several that reflects on the research undertaken into what makes some communities and some nations happier than others. This research begins with the principle that when people say they are generally happy or very happy in life, this is something that can be measured. Secondly, Layard looks at the major factors in life which contribute to happiness. The results are fascinating.

First, being happy seems to contribute directly to good health. Second, being rich doesn't make anyone happy. Many countries in the developing world with low income levels per capita are just as content as developed nations, and in some cases happier. Internationally, once people achieve an average income of about $15,000 per year (that's dollars, not pounds) anything they earn above that level doesn't make them any happier.

Layard defines his 'Big 7' factors that affect happiness. The first five are in order of importance:

1. **Family relationships** – countries with the highest rates of divorce and family break-up have relatively unhappy populations.

2. **Financial situation** – not earning enough for your needs, or feeling pressurized to earn competitively for reasons of status tends to lead to less happiness.

3. **Work** – being underemployed or economically inactive makes us unhappy; doing relatively fulfilling work acts as a positive. Layard writes: 'When people become unemployed, their happiness falls much less because of the loss of income than because of the loss of work itself.'

4. **Community and friends** – having active friendship groups and being involved in community activity and associations increases happiness.

5. **Health** – ill-health, particularly where it involves pain and distress, naturally leads to unhappiness.

6. **Personal freedom** – having some independence in our life decisions helps us to be happy.

7. **Personal values** – being of service to others, contributing to society and having a personal faith are all factors which increase happiness.

It's worth revisiting what Layard has to say about work:

'Work is vital, if that is what you want. But it is also important that the work is fulfilling. Perhaps the most important issue is the extent

to which you have control over what you do. There is a creative spark in each of us, and if it finds no outlet, we feel half-dead. This can be literally true: among British civil servants of any given grade, those who do the most routine work experience the most rapid clogging of the arteries.'

Richard Layard, Happiness – Lessons from a New Science,
Allen Lane 2005

The good, the bad and the just plain awful

What are the things at work that give you the greatest buzz? The sort of things you go home and talk about? Write them down. It's worth recording the good things. Take a blank piece of paper and divide it into three. Write down everything that you would include under each heading:

1. THE REALLY GOOD STUFF   Things you find stimulating and enjoyable

2. THINGS I COULD LIVE WITHOUT   When do you find work boring or dull?

3. THINGS I PUT UP WITH AT WORK THAT I NEED LIKE A HOLE IN THE HEAD   What aspects of work fill you with dread or loathing?

The following sets out some common statements or perceptions from people who were asked how happy they are at work. Not all of the statements will match your personal situation, and you may have your own that you would like to add. Which category in Table 2.1 describes you best?

Table 2.1   How happy are you in your career?

How you feel about work

A   **Dream job**
I can't wait to get into work. Work is the place where I grow and learn most, where I am set healthy challenges, where I am valued and appreciated. A great deal of fun and self-esteem are centred in my work, which fits my values, talents

and personality. I *know* that I make a difference. I express who I am in my job. The rewards are right, and I would be happy to be paid less if necessary. I love life, and love the part work plays in it.

B   Thumbs up

I enjoy work most of the time, but sometimes there are headaches and problems. My work feels useful and contributes to my self-esteem. My contribution is clear, acknowledged and significant. My career is a good match to my talents, personality and values. I am appreciated by others. I feel that I make a difference, and that I add something positive to the organization. I find supervision helpful, but my boss is more a mentor than a supervisor. I lead a satisfying career which contributes to all parts of my life.

C   Mustn't grumble

I accept the work I do. Sometimes I feel valued, other times exploited or ignored. Work is stable, largely unexciting, doesn't interfere with my inner life too much. New ways of doing things are sometimes discouraged. I may be in the right line of work, but in the wrong organization. I am valued for some of what I do, but not always the most important things.

D   Someone's got to do it

I work because I need to. Otherwise I don't feel I owe a great deal to my employer. Several parts of the job are unpleasant/boring/demeaning/pointless. Real life begins at 5 o'clock. I'm not learning anything. I try to make a contribution but sometimes hit a brick wall. Some of my best skills are getting rusty. Sometimes I feel I would just like a quiet life.

E   Wage slave

There are days I almost have to drag myself to work; every day and every moment is miserable. I feel a huge mismatch between the person I am and the person this job requires me to be. I feel trapped. Each day makes things seem worse. I take all my sick leave because the job makes me ill. At times it feels like I am just surviving.

Various surveys suggest that only 30% of people are in group A or B. If you're in box A, congratulations. Recognize what's good about your work and ensure that it remains that way. If you're in box E, again you're among about 10% of workers. Make a review of how you can change things. Soon. The thing about an unfulfilled life is the damage done by what's missing. Most of us are somewhere between B and D. Career transition should be about moving up the scale.

Nothing has a stronger influence psychologically on children than the unlived lives of their parents.

                                                                Carl Jung

YOUR WORLD VIEW

Careers specialists have long talked about *motivated skills*; in other words, the skills you relish using, the skills you would exercise for next to nothing, even for free. There's a huge difference between doing something because you know how and doing something because you actively choose to do so. That difference is the power of motivation. Motivation turns a task into a joy, an errand into a quest, a job into a vocation.

The key ingredient in your career exploration is the degree of motivation you apply to the process. *You get out what you put in*. Read that last sentence again. Your success in gaining a stunning career depends as much on your own personal motivation as it does on any other combination of factors, internal or external.

Where does that motivation come from? Think about your **world view**. Think about what makes up that picture. It contains your memories, your history, elements of the world views held by your parents, friends and loved ones. In it you'll find your preconceptions, your fears, your values. A world view is made up of sentences as well as pictures. We have an all-too familiar script running most of the time: 'charity begins at home', 'if you want a job doing properly, do it yourself', 'keep your cards close to your chest'. Look closely at the picture you hold of yourself, the script you run in your own personal soap opera. Do you see the glass as half full or half empty?

Ah, that depends .... And it does. It depends on the way *you* look. Look at the signals you receive during the course of a day. How many times do you receive praise and ignore it? How many times do you hear neutral or objective data and take it the wrong way? How often do you hear criticism and clutch it to yourself as the last, final and totally accurate picture of *you*? The reality is that most of us have an impressive talent: to ignore positive information, distort neutral information and attach ourselves to negative information.

Where you put the energy matters. If you put your energy into believing the glass is half empty, what you see is emptiness, absence, insufficiency. If you choose to put your energy into seeing the glass as half full, you will see fullness and abundance everywhere.

Information is neutral. But where do you put your energy and attention? You fill your personal bubble with evidence of what you lack: 'I can't do that ...', 'I've never been good at ...', 'Nobody's interested in me when I ...'. You have a natural, inexhaustible ability to hang on to these favourite ideas. Those who understand the secrets of motivation are generally masters of two areas of personal growth:

1. They know who they are, and what they are good at.

2. They know when to ignore negative data, when to accept a neutral picture as simply neutral, and when to remember and act upon all the good things they ever learned about themselves.

At this point you may be hearing two words in your head:

YES, BUT ...

About now the **YES, BUT** area of the brain is kicking in. We all do it. It's actually an identifiable part of the human psyche the American author Ned Herrmann called the *safekeeping self*. The safekeeping self is the senior committee member who faithfully attends every meeting in your brain and says: 'We've heard all this stuff before', 'It'll never fly', 'I'd be taking a risk', 'It might work for somebody else', 'Show me the statistics', 'it might work in London, but …'. Which all sounds rather like:

Everything that can be invented has been invented.

We should hold a special place in our hearts for the man who uttered that last sentence. His name was Charles H. Duell, Director of the US Patent Office. He said it in 1899.

'Yes, but' thinking is the biggest block to career transition. Saying 'Yes, but' is a good way of avoiding an issue and avoiding change: 'Yes, but I have to earn a living', 'Yes, but in the real world …'. It's often a sign that the speaker is not listening positively – it's a classic defence mechanism, a way of avoiding having to face issues.

Normal is getting dressed in clothes that you buy for work, driving through traffic in a car that you are still paying for, in order to get to the job that you need so you can pay for the clothes, car and the house that you leave empty all day in order to afford to live in it.

Ellen Goodman

PROBLEMS FOR THE CAREER DOCTOR

Time to discuss your various 'Yes, but' symptoms. The Career Doctor will see you now.

Too long in the same job

The 'same job' could have been a 20-year history of change, variety and development. We're not demotivated by being in one job or one organization. We're turned off when things start repeating themselves and we're not learning or changing.

Even if you're in a great job that you love doing, you may not want to do it forever. Most careers need a reboot from time to time.

The side benefits are good

In one firm an employee stayed on for several years because somebody in the office brought in an excellent cake every day. We all have our reasons for staying and our reasons for leaving. The million-dollar question is: are these the *real* reasons? People are very good at finding excuses for avoiding the real issues, or justifying decisions. If you find yourself saying 'the pension scheme/the medical insurance/the gym is so good …', then the question should be: *but is this why I'm here*? Side benefits go quickly in times of trouble.

Talk to people after they have retired. Do they talk about the salary and benefits, or do they talk about the good relationships, the fun, the excitement, the feeling of doing meaningful work? When you're on your deathbed, are you going to say 'I wish my pension had been just a bit bigger' or 'why did I waste 20 years in that office watching the clock?'

I'll stick it out

'The job's okay, and a lot of things are good about it, but …'. This general sense of dissatisfaction needs focus. Is it really the whole job that doesn't suit, or part of it? Is it just some of the people you work with? Are there problems elsewhere in your life (partner, health, family) and work provides a convenient dumping ground for your troubles?

The answer to these questions takes a little time to work out, but you can begin by asking:

▮ What parts of the job do I enjoy?

▮ What parts do I *really* enjoy? When does the time pass quickly?

▌ If I could change something using a magic wand, would it be the people, the place, the rewards, the tasks I do? Make a list, then look at what you can actually change, and be aware of the difference between what can be changed, and what can't.

A word of warning: it's all too easy to believe that the only solution to dissatisfaction at work is job change. Often all that work dissatisfaction shows you is that there's a mismatch between who you are and what you are doing. That mismatch shows, if not to ourselves, to others. But the real answer is **career growth**: moving towards a closer match between yourself and the work you do. Career growth may be something you can achieve exactly where you are already.

I'm too old

Yes, employers are wrong-headed about age. But time and time again they buy experience, know-how, reliability. Look at the information the employer is sending in the job description: do you hear steadiness, reliability or short-term energy? Try to match who you are and what you have to offer against the job. Look at Table 2.2 for a range of strategies for those who feel that age is a barrier.

Remember this: employers who discriminate on the grounds of age are either too young to appreciate that anyone can have an original idea over the age of 30 (so show them ...) or old and tired and assume that everyone over 40 is equally old and tired. If the employer wants a 21-year-old he can burn out in 2 years, do you want to be there anyway?

Table 2.2 Age and work: how big is the problem?

The negative side *The key facts on age and employment*	**The (more) positive side** *Ways of compensating by changing your approach or thinking*

Workers over 50 are now less likely to be working than they were 20 years ago. Few people now assume that they will stay in their present job until the age of 65. About one-third of people between the ages of 50 and 60 are unemployed or inactive, despite being in relatively good health.

The working population is ageing. There are fewer young people around. Four out of 10 workers nationally are over the age of 45. There are just not enough bright young things around. New legislation on age discrimination makes it harder for employers to screen out older workers.

Men are more likely than women to become economically inactive over the age of 55.

And how many of those men relied simply on physical fitness to achieve a living, and allowed themselves to be passive flotsam in the job market, employed one day, unemployed the next? Even in times of recession you can find stories of older workers who got back into doing worthwhile work. Seek out those people. Find out how they did it. You'll discover that it was a mix of determination and positive thinking.

Approximately 50% of men aged between 60 and 65 are not working.

Percentages? A proportion of people are always doing something or not doing something. Don't be a statistic.

A high proportion of workers are retiring before their company's normal retirement age.

... often because they have become tired and unhappy, and because they have stopped learning.

Employers think that younger people are more adaptable, learn more quickly and have more energy to dedicate to work.

OK, and statistically they will be more likely to drink to excess, have hangovers and decide to go off backpacking round Australia. Older workers are more reliable, steadier and, if they package themselves right, better able to offer a blend of learning and common sense.

Adaptability is something you claim and show evidence to support. Learning can be demonstrated by your current interests. All too many older workers are happy to say 'All this computer stuff is beyond me ...' and don't hear the door slamming shut.

There seems some evidence to suggest that older people are likely to be out of work if (a) they are in the bottom 25% of earners or (b) they are in the top 50% of earners and also in an occupational pension scheme.	... which shows that some age problems are simply economic, and some caused by employer pension policies, which sometimes make it more convenient to encourage early retirement as a comfortable way of 'downsizing'.
Many areas of work are perceived as 'young' jobs.	Age discrimination is unlawful in the UK, and a great many employers conform to equal opportunities policies. It's worth asking, explicitly, 'what is the likely age range for this post?'
Other research reflects a widespread belief that those close to retirement have less to lose through redundancy and job loss, and that the risk of displacement from work is higher among people who are older. In other words, workers over 45 are more vulnerable to job loss, and find it harder to get back into work.	Employers gain all kinds of irrational, negative pictures about all kinds of people: students, single mothers, vegetarians. The key thing is not to feed the flames of prejudice, but to concentrate on what you have to offer. Sometimes it's helpful specifically to address the age issue: 'What kind of experience

are you looking for?', 'How long is this project?', or even to ask specifically 'What's the *minimum* age/experience requirement for this job?'

Key advice for older workers

First of all, acknowledge that age discrimination is real. The reason for beginning there is that if you know something is real, you can begin to compensate. If you're not a natural with numbers, compensate by finding tools to help. Concentrate on who you are, and what makes you special.

Employers value a number of things that older workers have in abundance: experience, reliability (a 'safe pair of hands'), credibility, maturity, financial stability (you won't be asking for a pay rise every 6 months).

Here's some of the best advice around, from John Courtis, head of executive search and selection firm John Courtis & Partners, to whom I am grateful for permission to print the following from his Candidate Newsletter:

Too young? Too old? Does your age matter?

▪ Only if you keep on about it

▪ Only if you look it

▪ Only if you bring it up and apologize for it in your covering letter

▪ Only if the photo you've attached to your CV makes you look significantly older/younger than the chronological date would suggest

▪ And last – only if you don't distract the reader from it with all the *good* things you have to offer – recent relevant achievements, unique selling points, etc.

I don't have the qualifications

Formal qualifications are often far less relevant than people think, particularly in flexible environments like Britain and the USA. Two considerations here: there are now so many young people obtaining degrees, diplomas and certificates that employers can't tell one from another, and they have no idea whether the qualification equates to workplace performance.

If the qualification is a legal or safety requirement, then get it, or a recognized equivalent. But it's always worth investigating the alternatives. Find out what other ways there are to get in. Can you train on the job? Can you buy the training somewhere? What kind of parallel experience might be accepted?

Where an employer mentions a specific qualification you don't have, don't despair, and don't send in your application anyway, saying nothing, hoping that your lack of a Certificate in Astrological Science won't be noticed. Ask yourself, 'why do they need this? – what problem will it solve?' – and then address the issue directly by communicating what you know and what you can do: your answer to the problem posed by this job.

I'm not IT literate

Do something about it. At one time using a PC, the Internet and email was a specialized skill. Now it's common currency. And it's not rocket science either. As a minimum target, get yourself connected and acquire an email address (get a friend to set it up – that part is a real headache, but using it is much easier than setting the timer on your video).

I'd need to retrain/go back to university/college

This is a great 'Yes, but', because it's a logical brick wall: the only way I can get a great future is if I stop working (to study or retrain full-time). Not so. There are a million and one choices in education today: part-time study, open and distance learning. Bookshops have miles of texts telling you how to do things. Find a motivated person and he or she will be learning something all the time: about computers, about gardening, wine, music, maps, and so on.

I don't have the time or energy to study. Is that true? If the job you do takes so much out of you and leaves nothing left for learning, maybe it's the wrong job, or maybe you're doing the right job the wrong way?

I'll never earn what I earn here

The trouble with the rat race is that even if you win, you're still a rat.
Lily Tomlin

This one's the kiss of death, because it's really saying 'I'm over-paid here and nobody else will let me get away with it'. This is usually very wrong-headed. Very few people are overpaid for more than a short period. Whatever you're earning (or have earned) is a reflection of what someone, somewhere, feels is the justified cost of your presence and activity.

Being found out

It's surprising how many people in senior jobs share a common fear: that they are only pretending to be good enough to do the job, and one day they'll be found out. It's known as the **Impostor Syndrome**. Their boss will say: 'OK, we know it's been a big pretence. Just leave now and we'll say nothing more about it.' Insecurity is everywhere.

I can't get motivated to make the change I need

You don't have to make a big change on day one, but you *do* need to do something. It's true that sometimes we can't get round to doing the very thing that we know will make life better. Why do we fail to take the first step? If it's a direction you know you want to take, then the usual answer is fear of failure, which can include fear of rejection. There's a simple trick I use with many clients: imagine you were making enquiries for someone else. A colleague has offered you several thousand pounds to find *her* ideal career path. If you accepted that brief you wouldn't be going back every five minutes saying 'this won't work for you', 'this isn't as exciting as I thought' or 'this is a difficult sector to get into'. You'd keep exploring, keep looking for variations and angles, press on by asking questions like 'what else is there?', 'who else could I talk to?', and 'what are the unconventional ways into this field?'.

I don't interview well

What does *interviewing well* really mean? If it means that you're negative, that you talk yourself out of every job you apply for, then this isn't a matter of technique, but just a trick you play. The trick is this: you think you'll fail, so you set the game out to ensure that you do. That way you won't be disappointed. Employers in general buy experience, but they also love enthusiasm. That's not the same as false confidence, but conveying a simple statement: *I like what I do. I do it well. I can do it here, for you.* Chapter 12 has a wide range of tips.

I'm just waiting for the phone to ring

It's your life. If the phone rings, it's because somebody needs you to solve a problem. Their problem. Getting your career right is nobody else's problem.

EXERCISE 2.1 – UNDERSTAND YOUR CONSTRAINTS

We all have constraints, but each of us thinks that our constraints are uniquely limiting. Tick the constraints that you feel apply to you.

- ☐ I am too old
- ☐ I am underqualified
- ☐ My experience is all in one industry
- ☐ Travel to work distance
- ☐ Travel as part of the job
- ☐ Nights away from home
- ☐ Lack of information about the job market
- ☐ The stigma of unemployment
- ☐ No clear career goals
- ☐ Financial commitments
- ☐ Family/personal problems
- ☐ Fear of approaching people
- ☐ Few measurable achievements
- ☐ Attitudes/needs of family members
- ☐ Lack of confidence selling myself in person
- ☐ I worry about taking risks
- ☐ Worry that I will repeat old problems

- ☐ Worry that I will be out of work for a long time
- ☐ Fear of employer's attitude to redundancy or unemployment
- ☐ I have health problems
- ☐ Lack of up-to-date skills
- ☐ I am out of touch with the market
- ☐ Fear of rejection
- ☐ Lack of relevant qualifications
- ☐ Worry about having to retrain/go back to full-time study
- ☐ My job search to date hasn't worked
- ☐ Don't want to make the wrong decision at my time of life
- ☐ Want to get a job that looks good on my CV
- ☐ I want a safe job
- ☐ I have never had to apply for a job before
- ☐ I don't interview well

Look at the constraints you have ticked. Take a highlighter pen and mark the ones which you think are most critical or most limiting. Record against each one a time when you overcame this constraint in the past, and the steps you can see to help you to overcome this barrier in the future. If you feel you have constraints that you can't overcome, that's a good reason to find help.

'MUST DO' LIST

☑ Career problems are sometimes concrete, but usually strategies for avoiding the issue of change. What are your favourite 'Yes, but' defences?

☑ You can be happy at work. What would be the first step you could take to achieve that? How would your friends and colleagues notice the difference?

☑ Look at your CV, your interview style, your attitude to work. You complain that employers see negative things about you. How many of these messages are actually composed and delivered by you?

Where Next After Finishing Your Studies?

This chapter looks at ways of:

❚ Using this book if you are leaving school, college or university soon

❚ Building on your academic achievement

❚ Composing a CV when you have little or no work experience

❚ Translating what you know and can do into employer language

Of course, it is very important to be sober when you take an exam. Many worthwhile careers in the street-cleansing, fruit-picking and subway-guitar-playing industries have been founded on a lack of understanding of this simple fact.

Terry Pratchett

A 10-STEP CHECKLIST FOR SCHOOL LEAVERS CONSIDERING NEXT STEPS

1. Choose your subjects for further study carefully. Avoid being press-ganged into a subject because someone else thinks it's a good idea.

2. Areas of further study should meet two benchmarks: (a) the qualification will be a reasonable stepping stone, and (b) you will be motivated to study the topic (this works best if you really enjoy what you are studying).

3. Accept all ideas for career pathways gratefully, but make up your own mind based on evidence. Talk to real people in real jobs. Ask around: family, parents of friends, anyone you know in the world of work.

4. Where your studies are related to work, use them as a platform for your investigation. Most organizations will let you speak to some one if you are carrying out some research.

5. Take work experience and short-term work assignments seriously – write down the skills you use and what you have learned.

6. Be very clear about your qualifications – why did you study them, what are they, what did they cover, and what are your grades? BUT when you apply for a job list them *after* your skills and work experience, however limited that is.

7. Stuck for a career idea? Use this book to help, but begin by looking at two big areas of life for clues:

   ▪ what you enjoy doing (how do you spend your free time? what activities motivate you?)

   ▪ what do you enjoy thinking/talking/learning about?

8. If you are totally stuck about career choice, look at what you love doing and try to find the opportunity to try it out on a work experience basis.

9. Use temporary work as a way of gaining skills and relevant experience.

10. Don't accept secondhand information – from websites, teachers, family, careers advisers – find out for yourself.

'I DON'T KNOW WHAT KIND OF WORK I WANT TO DO'

If you have recently qualified, or you are thinking about your future while still in full-time education, you may feel you are facing a bewildering range of choices regarding possible jobs and careers. Your problem may in fact be that you don't know enough about work to know which parts you are going to dislike. You may have little work experience, or you may feel that your experience is not appropriate or useful to the new career you are hoping to begin.

On the other hand, many people in their 40s and 50s say 'I wish I'd thought more carefully about career choice when I was young'. It's up to you. If you add up the number of hours, days and weeks you put into achieving qualifications, it's rather surprising how little attention people give to the question 'what kind of work would really suit me?'

Begin with some background thinking:

■ Look at all the subjects that have interested you, and translate them into potential fields of work using Chapters 9 and 10.

■ Look at all your experience of work to date. What has motivated you or excited you? Where is your sense of *flow*? (See Chapter 4.)

■ Look at the subjects you have just studied. What would you like to know more about? What skills have you developed while studying?

■ Conduct an audit: what do you actually know about work? How can you find out more? Who can you talk to? Appendix 1 shows you how you can use REVEAL interviews to help.

Next, *think research rather than job search*. Don't miss out on the obvious sources of information:

■ Your university careers service or any of the organizations offering specialist careers guidance to young people and adults

■ Lecturers and subject specialists.

■ Text resources, including the hundreds of career books and guides to specific occupations which are available.

■ Reference libraries (the staff can be enormously helpful).

■ Websites relating to employers, industry sectors and career entry.

■ Professional and trade associations (see the website listings in Appendix 3 for ways in).

Next, undertake the kind of investigation that most people leaving full-time education don't do:

▌ Talk to students a year ahead of you who have found work.

▌ Ask around – friends, parents of your friends, former teachers and lecturers.

▌ Talk to people who have employed you in the past.

The first item on this list may sound painfully obvious, but very few *current* students make use of alumni associations. Talking to someone who has qualified in your subject and is now in work can help you enormously in your thinking, especially if you are trying hard to work out (a) if you will enjoy the work they do and (b) how you can persuade an employer that you have transferable skills.

WHAT CHOICES DO I HAVE APART FROM FINDING A JOB?

Undertaking 2 or 3 years' **further study** may seem like the most comfortable option. Indeed, many students choose this as the 'default' mode, but is this the right step? Taking a higher qualification can give you a late start on the salary ladder, but is it an essential requirement for the career you have in mind? Are you continuing simply because you have been offered a grant or a place, or because you don't know what else to do? Ask yourself the real motives for continuing your studies.

Taking time out may also appeal. Again, the question is whether you want to delay your career start merely to indulge yourself, to put off a decision, or whether there are things you really want to do. There is probably no other time in your life when you will be able to travel with so few restrictions, but think hard about what you will learn from the experience. Employers need to see the relevance of your year out, and what you learned from the experience. Sometimes you can successfully combine travel with work.

Thinking rather than drifting

Whatever your career stage, it's vitally important to be active rather than passive in your job search. If you are entirely passive, taking what the labour market offers, it is rather like planning a long journey by turning up at a bus station and jumping on the first bus to arrive. If you start that way then job change often becomes a question of jumping on whatever vehicle happens to come along at a time when you feel dissatisfied.

Your first full-time job makes a big impact on your career. Many people take 'fill-in' jobs after qualifying. The danger is that this kind of work can quickly lead to the idea that 'this is all there is' or 'this is what work is like'. You may develop the idea that the work you do will never be linked in any way to your studies. 'Fill-in' jobs can quickly become permanent posts unless you keep your goals in mind.

Ideas are powerful. Career counsellors will tell you that one of the difficulties they have in dealing with young people or those with little work experience is that, essentially, all work looks the same. Very often it's only after some work experience that you get a 'feel' for the kind of work you would really like to do.

The advantage of traditional graduate trainee programmes was they allowed entrants to gain experience of many different parts of a business before choosing to specialize. The number of schemes has decreased significantly in the past decade, and at the same time research from organizations such as the Work Foundation indicates that on average workers have become less satisfied with their work and less productive. Do you want to be one of those casualties of work? Assuming that you don't, how can you replicate the experience of a good graduate entry programme; in other words, how can you give yourself the widest choice in work?

YOUR SKILLS KITBAG

Table 3.1 lists a range of career management and self-reliance skills seen by employers as vital for workers competing in the twenty-first century labour market. The information comes from the Association of Graduate Recruiters, but an understanding of these skills and qualities is useful to anyone beginning a career.

Table 3.1 Career management and effective learning skills

Self-awareness	Being able to identify your own skills, values, interests and strengths, seek feedback from others, and seek opportunities for personal growth.
Self-promotion	Being able to define and promote your own agenda, i.e. actively communicating your 'message' (see Chapter 7 on presentation statements).
Exploring and creating opportunities	Being able to identify, create, investigate and seize opportunities.
Action planning	Goal-setting, organizing your time effectively, and preparing contingency plans along the way to achieving goals and targets.
Networking	Being able to define, develop and maintain the support network for advice and information.
Matching and decision making	Finding a match between opportunities you meet and your own core skills and knowledge; making informed decisions based on constraints and opportunities.
Negotiation	Negotiating the psychological contract to achieve win/win.

Political awareness	Being aware of hidden tensions and power struggles within organizations (sometimes defined as spotting the most likely person to stab you in the back).
Coping with uncertainty	Adapting goals and your mindset in the light of changing circumstances.
Development focus	Being committed to lifelong learning and your own personal development.
Transfer skills	Applying your skills, and communicating them, to new contexts. See 'Translation', below.
Self-confidence	Having an underlying confidence in your abilities, in terms of both past success and your innate qualities.

Adapted from *Skills for Graduates in the 21st Century*, reprinted with permission from the Association of Graduate Recruiters.

AGR Chief Executive Carl Gilleard says: 'We ask our members what skills they are looking for in graduates when they're recruiting. And not surprisingly, top of the list, come interpersonal skills and the ability to communicate effectively, the ability to work in teams, and customer awareness. We also find that employers very much look for candidates who have had work experience; that carries a high premium these days. And let's not forget the old-fashioned attributes of enthusiasm, motivation and commitment all of these things still carry a lot of weight with employers.'

HOW TO WRITE A CV IF YOU HAVE LITTLE OR NO WORK EXPERIENCE

When you have just qualified, putting good-quality evidence in your CV is a tough job. Those leaving the world of education have some perception gaps about their 'offer'. You may have a fairly good idea of your strengths, personal preferences and values. However, you probably haven't yet really understood how to communicate your skills and achievements to an employer.

Your achievements can range from building a tree house to backpacking in the Himalayas – not just working activities. Now look for the *skills* and *personality traits* that you demonstrate. Remember that the new economy is looking for flexibility, resilience and imagination, as well as traditional skills and know-how. Try to say something user friendly and interesting about your main qualification. A subject title is rarely helpful to an employer. A recruiter makes assumptions about the usefulness of your qualification unless you specifically state what you most enjoyed about it, what special projects you undertook and what you got out of it. The **Skill Clips** exercise in Chapter 7 can help.

Look at your activities outside study. Perhaps you organized complicated or exciting social events, competitions or sporting activities, or you may have been a member of a society or club. Think about the transferable skills that you acquired from these experiences, and make sure that they are mentioned in your CV.

Some academic subjects are, sadly, off-putting to potential employers. Think about ways of selling the subject, for example explaining why the topics you have studied are relevant to a modern workplace. Even if you have done something fairly obscure and academic, you will have gained considerable experience of researching, organizing and analysing data, consulting experts and presenting information concisely and coherently in speech and in writing. Table 3.2 offers some advice on ways of composing a winning message.

Table 3.2 Ten steps to a winning message when seeking work when leaving full-time education

1 Experience	An employer is trying to measure potential, but provide what information you can about

	relevant experience (e.g. work, travel, time out). Indicate what kind of challenges you faced, what you learned and what you achieved.
2 Skills	Be honest, which means neither bragging nor hiding your light under a bushel. Identify your skills and state your level of competence. Give examples of what you have done with these skills (e.g. leading an expedition of 10 people for a 20-mile trek).
3 Key achievements	Make sure that you include achievements. Think about your accomplishments in different contexts: study, work, leisure time, voluntary activities. Try to present your achievements in interesting terms, explaining them as mini-narratives if necessary (see Chapter 7 for further details).
4 Qualifications	Explain, translate, communicate. Don't assume that an employer is automatically interested in your academic achievements. Don't overemphasize poor results.
5 Education and continuing professional development	Don't forget to include details about non-academic courses and training, even if they are uncertificated. If you have the skills but not the qualifications, give an indication of what you have achieved with them (e.g. producing a complex spreadsheet).
6 Work history	What did you actually do? What problems did you solve? Look at any work you have ever done and find a way to communicate the skills you used and the contribution you made.
7 Support skills	Think about the support skills you can offer, and an employer's expectations (e.g. IT, word processing, customer service or sales skills). Don't miss out anything, particularly IT skills. Indicate your standard of competence.

8 Fields of work	Work out what kind of work interests you. Communicate enthusiasm to employers: show them that you really want to work in their field, not that they happen to be the first to have a vacancy.
9 Interests	Include a good range. An employer won't expect you to have a long work history, but will expect you to be a rounded person with an interesting life outside work. Focus on interests and activities that include other people or develop skills that may be relevant to work.
10 Profile	This is a short paragraph of no more than four sentences saying what sort of role you have in mind, your current role or position, your key experience to date and what you can offer an employer in broad terms. This will form the first part of your CV. Avoid flowery adjectives or claims you can't support. See Chapter 17 for outline CV advice, and look at the range of CV models presented in *Why You? – CV Messages To Win Jobs*.

TRANSLATION

The single biggest problem with CVs of university or college leavers is a failure to translate qualities, know-how and experience into terms that are meaningful to an employer. This isn't just a problem for people leaving full-time education; it's very difficult for people to leave teaching, the health service or the armed forces for exactly the same reason. You find yourself immersed in a particular language, and then fail to perceive the need to help others to understand what these terms mean.

I sometimes use the term 'bridge thinking'. What you essentially want a recruiter to do is to form a bridge between your experience and the world of the hiring company. You want an employer to see not just skills, but transferable skills. You have to do the bridge thinking for the other person. For example, if you simply write that you produced a 6000-word dissertation on fish farming, you may get a fairly blank response. If, however, you talk about the problems of gathering data, interviewing people, keeping up with the latest developments in your subject area, and working under pressure to achieve the project by a fixed deadline, then your interviewer starts to get interested. You have started to talk the same language.

BECOME HUNGRY FOR EVIDENCE OF YOUR EMPLOYABILITY

You will find that your job search will be easier if you are able to offer concrete evidence of skills and achievements. Increasing numbers of students are working while studying. Sometimes this is just during vacations, sometimes students work up to 20 hours a week or more during term-time. If you find it difficult to gain paid work experience in your chosen field of work, consider working as a volunteer. There are few formal internships in the UK, but that does not mean that you cannot suggest one. Several of my clients have gained crucial work experience by working for a short, intense period for nothing. However, if you work for nothing, always ask for something in exchange, even if it is only a learning experience, a reference, or some concrete feedback of how you have done and how you can progress in the future.

KEEP A RECORD

Work experience isn't just for your bank balance. Build up your own personal portfolio of what you have done, including details of your role, the company, the contribution you made and where you made a difference.

Look in detail at all the times you have had exposure to work:

■ placements during a sandwich course

■ overseas work or study placement

■ work during term-time

■ work experience elements in a course of study

■ vacation work

■ workplace visits or tours.

RETURNING TO WORK AFTER TAKING TIME OUT TO STUDY

Those who have taken a career break to take a full-time course usually need to think carefully when trying to return to the workplace. Taking time out to study places a gap in your CV, and doesn't always communicate employability; for a start, you have to convince an employer that you really are motivated to return to paid employment.

The key thing to remember is that you need short, focused answers to three questions:

1. Why did you decide to give up work to take this qualification?

2. What did you get out of it?

3. What do you hope to do next as a direct result of your studies?

If you fail to give an adequate answer to Question 1, a recruiter starts to worry that you make random decisions in your career, or that you might be in danger of becoming a life-long student. Question 2 requires you to think about *translation* (see above), but also requires you to talk with enthusiasm about what you enjoyed whilst studying (after all, if you didn't enjoy it, why did you do it?). The third question requires you to communicate a clear, straightforward data-burst about the way this recent experience adds to your CV and has helped to reshape your career path.

Special advice to holders of MBAs

Those who have taken time out to study for an MBA often need particular help. This is ironic, because an MBA is a clear badge of employability.

Business Schools, in order to persuade you to part with a large quantity of money, will make huge claims about their alumni and the kinds of jobs they have acquired. It's easy to feel persuaded that having an MBA is an instant passport to success.

When MBAs come to the end of a very intensive course they know that they have to hit the deck running and find a job. One problem they face is that the work they do next may not be as challenging and demanding as the course they have just completed. I have met MBAs who, as part of their course, have worked alongside Main Board Directors of Blue Chip European companies. Their course of study has given them this unique access, but one of the things the new MBAs have to get used to is the fact that they are unlikely to work at this level immediately upon qualifying.

The next problem (based on feedback from a number of recruiters) is that MBAs assume that everything about their qualification is clear. We're back to the basic questions above, but this time the questions (whether spoken or implied) are slightly different:

1. Why did you decide to suspend your career and spend a large amount of money to study for an MBA?

2. What did you learn on your MBA that has added to your skill set?

3. How do you hope to use your MBA next?

4. *Why you*, in a market flooded with MBAs?

In this case Question 1 has more impact, simply because of the high cost of paying for an MBA, and also because of the greater risk to a high-flying career.

Question 2 again requires *translation*, but this time you should have pre-rehearsed, impressive answers about particular projects and achievements, particularly where they relate to work you have done with real organizations.

The third question needs to be highly focused indeed: where did you want the MBA to take you? Unclear answers around this topic sound very weak indeed – why have you spent so much time and money doing something with an unclear outcome in mind? Recruiters often have a prejudice that fresh MBAs don't stay in organizations for long. This isn't just based on a hunch: statistics from Business Schools regularly show us that a high proportion of MBAs change career shortly after graduating.

Finally, to Question 4. Why you? You'll have a hard job selling your MBA just on the reputation of your Business School. Although this sometimes works, you have to be able to communicate what you learned, and how your experience allows you to offer something different from all the other candidates out there with exactly the same qualification from Business Schools all over the world.

Recruiters will tell you that too many MBAs at interview just don't have the answers to these questions in a well-constructed, packaged response. You have to remember that the person interviewing you might love to have your opportunity to study full-time, or might have bad experience of MBAs (as employ-ees, or as management consultants). Since there are more than a few MBAs out there with enlarged egos, you might also be considered to be a know-it-all before you get to a job interview.

'MUST DO' LIST: HOW TO USE THIS BOOK IF YOU HAVE JUST QUALIFIED

Think about how you are going to choose your career. If you have no idea about what kind of work you would like to do, use the various exercises in this book, particularly in Chapter 10. Draw up a shortlist of ideas, and then talk to as many people as you can. This is more important now than at any stage of your working life. Find out what other people like you have gone into, and ask them how they got there, what they enjoy about it, and what kind of applicants do well in the selection process.

To work smarter at your career, start with the principle of *leverage*. A small amount of time now spent seriously thinking about career possibilities will have an enormous impact in your future life. What negative messages are holding you back at the moment? How many of them come from other people? How many of those thoughts are accurately informed by objective information about the real marketplace? How are you going to create real ideas about your career future?

Examine your **Career Hot Buttons** (Chapter 5) and draw up your personal wish list. You may find it important to think about the likely values of organizations you will be talking to.

What do you have to offer? Look seriously at your skills. Build carefully – based on what you have done and the work that becomes available to you in the short term. Catalogue your skills and achievements. There is an argument that almost any kind of work experience is valuable at this stage for you to experiment and work out where your skills really lie.

Use the **field choice** exercises in this book to help generate possible pathways. Don't give up too early on career choice, and don't shelve ideas until you have taken the opportunity to talk to real people about real jobs. Research what's out there, otherwise you're planning a journey with blank maps.

Prepare now for **interviews**. Don't believe that interviews are a matter of luck. Prepare. Work out what the employer is really looking for, and work hard to communicate your strengths and your enthusiasm.

Thinking Around Corners

CHAPTER 4

This chapter looks at the following areas:

▋ How you normally solve problems

▋ Breaking out of A–Z thinking

▋ Aiming for career breakthrough

▋ Moving towards positive solutions

The most successful people are those who do all year long what they would otherwise do in their summer vacation.

Mark Twain

PROBLEM SOLVING, AND WHAT GOES WRONG

How can you solve the problem of your career? Well, if you use the strategies you have learned so far in your life, you'll probably try a structured approach such as undertaking research and working out possibilities logically and systematically. Such *structured* approaches usually rely on what you have learned about organizing information and ideas. We categorize problems. We write out lists. We prioritize. We time plan. We write out pros and cons. That's a sound, business-like way of working things out, isn't it?

A–Z thinking

Very few of us are taught that there are many different ways of thinking. In school and in work we learn *straight-line thinking*, a logical progression from one step to the next. This is the mindset that says every book must be read from front to back, from A to Z. From problem to solution: this was the language of a great deal of post-1945 management training: analyse the problem and work out a logical sequence of actions to form a solution.

Businesses all over the world are discovering that this kind of thinking doesn't help in every situation. Sometimes, survival depends on thinking more imaginatively. Many businesses have taken non-linear thinking to new heights: they turn problems on their heads. They seek innovative solutions. They invent new concepts, not just new products. In the twenty-first century, this is the kind of thinking to apply to our working lives.

This might be about being just a little less subject to tunnel vision. Accept that you can come up with new ideas for your future, and just try things out. For some it's about being open to *inspiration*. When you are inspired something larger than you moves within, whether that's the spirit of God, the spirit of life or something untapped in the human mind. How are you going to plan to be inspired? This sounds absurd, like planning to be spontaneous. You *can* plan inspiration, in the sense that you can open yourself up to possibilities, and you *can* learn to use both conscious and unconscious techniques to teach you how to break down barriers and begin to grow.

VARIETIES OF CREATIVE THINKING

Chapter 1 introduced you to the fact that everyone has their own form of creativity. However, it's important to remember that there are several kinds of creative thinking. Some of them come naturally to some people, but most can be nurtured or actively learned, as Figure 4.1 shows.

Straight-line creativity
This is step-by-step, detailed, methodical. It's fairly close to A–Z thinking, but ensures that you don't jump to one immediate conclusion. It's about defining a problem and looking for a variety of effective outcomes. This kind of creativity is great for questions such as 'who can I talk to about physiotherapy?' or 'what should I remember to take to the interview?' It can be done alone or in groups.

Used in career decisions it ensures that you use research, investigation and the full range of tools and techniques available to you.

Provoked creativity
This derives largely from the work of Edward de Bono, who even invented a new word for the purpose: *po* (read 'Serious Creativity'). The idea is that you can use an unexpected and unrelated prompt or *provocation* to make the mind switch gear: this may be an analogy, a metaphor, a word chosen at random or a picture. For example, think of your favourite pop song. What do the lyrics of that song make you think about? How can that help to solve your problem or create a new approach? Provoked creativity can be learned, and can be used by individuals or groups.

Used in career decisions it helps you to make unexpected connections. It's great for exploring fields, and for overcoming the 'Yes, but' barriers described in Chapter 2.

Freestyle creativity
This is free-flowing, fast, exciting. It relies on open-ended, **discontinuous thinking**: What else? What other ways are there of looking at this? What happens if I turn the problem on its head? Examples include brainstorming and idea creation. This kind of thinking tends to work best with other people to bounce your ideas off. This is the kind of thinking found in organizations who claim to be 'creative'.

Used in career decisions it generates positive possibilities and connections, and great ideas for researching jobs, fields, possible employers, etc.

Flash creativity
Sometimes known as 'Aha!' or 'Eureka!' moments, these are times when you get a sudden insight or moment of illumination. These often happen at a time when we are doing or thinking something entirely unrelated to the problem at hand, possibly having a bath or digging the garden. Flash creativity results in totally new ideas, approaches, products and ideas that did not exist before. There are no steps, no rules, no predictable outcomes. One way of aiding the process, however, is to feed your favoured natural intelligences (see Chapter 8 – Who Are You?)

Used in career decisions this kind of thinking occurs rarely, but the vital thing is to recognize the possibilities in the daydream, and test them out using one of the other forms of creative thinking.

Combine and conquer
It's important to realize that these kinds of creative thinking are not exclusive; they work best in combination with each other. Brainstorm possibilities using freestyle creativity. Use provoked thinking if you get stuck. Explore the range of positive practical outcomes using straight-line creativity. Reflect on a problem unconsciously by doing something that engages other parts of your brain: jogging, listening to a piece of music, stripping down an engine… (see Exercise 10.2 on discontinuous thinking).

Figure 4.1 Different styles of creative thinking

Go with the flow

Psychologist Mihaly Csikszentmihalyi coined the term **'flow'** to describe a state of existence you reach at times when you are totally absorbed in an enjoyable and fulfilling activity. Csikszentmihalyi describes nine characteristics of enjoyment, outlined in Figure 4.2.

FLOW

You find 'flow' in your work when...

1. There are clear goals every step of the way

2. There is immediate feedback to one's actions
   (i.e. we know how well we are doing)

3. There is a balance between challenges and skills
   (our opportunities and our skills are well matched)

4. Action and awareness are merged
   (our concentration is entirely focused on what we are doing)

5. Distractions are excluded from consciousness

6. There is no worry of failure

7. Self-consciousness disappears
   (we are too absorbed to worry about protecting our ego)

8. The sense of time becomes distorted
   (hours may pass in what seems like minutes)

9. The activity becomes autotelic
   (autotelic means 'an end in itself'. What Csikszentmihalyi means by this is that, as our skills increase, we begin to enjoy whatever produces this experience. With most artistic, sporting or musical activity, and some projects in all fields, the activity is an end in itself. We do it because we enjoy the feeling)

Adapted from Mihaly Csikszentmihalyi's *Creativity: Flow and the Psychology of Discovery and Invention*.

Figure 4.2   Flow

Getting unstuck

First, review where you feel a sense of dissatisfaction at work. Perhaps it's about knowing you could do more, or you would like to be valued more. A feeling that you don't quite match the life you're leading. A vague sense that there is more to life than this, that your work should have some meaning ….

Having got to this point, it's quite common for people to feel stuck in a rut. The worst kind of rut is the **velvet rut**: you hate its confines, but it's just too comfortable to move. You may get channelled or stuck in your ways, not just in work, but stuck in your thought processes, your career planning. You know that something needs to change, but what? What's needed is breakthrough thinking, something to take you from where you are to the next stage. You need to think up ideas.

The best way to get a good idea is to get lots of ideas.
Linus Pauling, Nobel prize winning scientist

There are a few ground rules for idea building:

■ Believe that the solution to your career block exists, either within you or somewhere out there.

■ Allow yourself to generate a range of ideas, without self-criticism.

■ Learn how to focus on both questions and solutions.

■ Don't restrict yourself to tools that you find easiest or the most comfortable. Stretch yourself.

■ Believe in your ability to succeed. Self-belief is vital.

Rule 1: **Behaviour follows belief**. The greatest barriers between you and an inspired career are not in the marketplace or on your CV, but in your mind. And if getting your ideal career requires positive thinking, then getting the ideas to put your career plan together takes even more; it's vital that you learn to accept your brain's own ability to create ideas, possibilities, connections. Accept that this is not only a natural gift for the chosen few, but (as thousands of businesses have discovered over the past 30 years) something you can practise and train your mind to do.

It's often said that the creative mind can hold contradictory ideas at the same time. So to Rule 2: **Belief follows behaviour**. This is certainly true in the very first stages of working on your self-belief. Sometimes the thing that works is to act and behave as if you are already successful. Walk the walk, talk the talk, and something happens – you physically act your way into a new way of looking at yourself. That's why it's easier to have authority if you are dressed professionally, and why people are more assertive on the telephone when they stand up.

Dick Bolles, author of *What Color is Your Parachute?*, has a wonderful saying: 'It is easier to act your way into a new way of thinking than to think your way into a new way of acting.' This has all kinds of implications. For example, if you have to make a public presentation, then one strategy is to act, walk and talk as if you already have the full attention of your audience. If you act confident or proficient, eventually you become it.

Finding new life in the old clichés

Too many businesses misuse the idea of creativity, and pay lip service to the idea of genuinely open thinking. Even the word 'creative' can become a cliché.

Clichés have their usefulness. 'Thinking outside the box' was a term used in the advertising industry to think outside the rectangular frame of an advertising billboard. 'Pushing the envelope' comes from the field of aviation. The 'envelope' is the box-like shape on a graph representing an aeroplane's maximum speed and range. Behind the tired language lie some very real business concepts.

What happens when there is a mismatch between your talents and your work? For creatures other than us humans, the answer to this question is extinction. Because we are so adaptable, we survive, but at a terrible cost. What gets extinguished is the pure joy of doing something that comes perfectly naturally. The further you get from fully expressing your talents and abilities, the less likely it is that you will enjoy your day on the job.

Nicholas Lore

CAREER BREAKTHROUGH TOOLS

Here's a range of tools from different sources that work well to help you to achieve career breakthrough.

Know where you're going

No, this isn't a reversion to straight-line thinking – all that objective-setting stuff. But it is about setting goals. Trainers talk about the importance of 'big hairy audacious goals', goals that are larger than life. Stephen Covey's book *The Seven Habits of Highly Effective People* advises us to 'begin with the end in mind' – set long-term goals you intend to reach.

Distinguish between goals and dreams. We're all great at having 'safe' dreams – ideas we like to play with, assured that we will never have to do anything about them. Goals are things we can do something about. For some people dreams become goals when logical/planning thinking is applied to them: 'what do I do next?'. However it's important to remember the dream as well, or the original impulse is lost.

Set real goals

Real goals are ideas that require a first step. Your goal might be to be self-employed within 3 years. It can remain a goal until you retire, or you can take the first step – an informational interview, perhaps (see Appendix 1).

It's a remarkable fact that goes against all logic, but every moti-vational trainer in the world will tell you the same thing: once you have decided on a goal, write it down. There seems a fair amount of evidence that it significantly increases your chances of achieving it.

Even if it's true that most career development is too much about action and not enough about reflection, it's vital to move on from reflecting and planning to actually *doing*. Set real goals and plan your first step.

Whether you think you can or you can't, you're right.

Henry Ford

Take happiness seriously

If you have reached career crisis, you'll already be in tune with this point. It's fairly central. If you don't believe in being happy, you probably don't believe in enjoyable work.

Theologian Sarah Maitland says that the word 'joy' comes from the same source as 'jewel'. We all seek some kind of hidden treasure in life – that missing 'something'. Often all we need is a better search method.

DIY

A huge jump in understanding demonstrated in career clients is that they, and only they, are responsible for their happiness.

Try a change of vocabulary. Describe the glass as half full, not half empty. Practise a register shift, from No to **Yes**.

The language of NO	The language of YES
It'll never work	Let's look at our alternatives
It's how I am: I was born that way	I can try a different approach

She makes me behave like that	I control my own feelings
It's against the rules	I'll invent a new rulebook
I'm forced to	I will choose
It's just not me	What shall I try next?
In the real world …	I make my world real by …
Another mistake	How interesting …
If only …	Let's try …
Never	It's all experimental

Stick to your guns

The key word here is 'integrity', which isn't just about doing the right thing, but *wholeness*. Once you know who you are and what you have to offer, try to resist offers that really don't match that discovery. I work with clients on the 70% principle. This is measured by drawing up your wish list in terms of work values, career hot buttons and the skills you would like to exercise, and then comparing it with the employer's stated wish list in the job description or advertisement. If there is a 70% overlap between their list of needs and wishes and a job opportunity, there's enough for it to be a healthy stepping stone. If not, watch out.

Look for synergy

It's a habit of life: look for connections. Carl Jung talked of *synchronicity*, a sense of things coming together in a pattern of significant coincidences. Those of faith may call them *Godincidences*, but you don't need to have strongly defined beliefs to become aware of synchronicity. Once you start to make connections, patterns in life start to emerge, and you become more aware of synergy. At a most basic level, the more you discover about yourself, the more you discover that many others around you are on a similar journey, with anxieties very similar to your own. Such people make good support partners.

EXERCISE 4.1 – SETTING GOALS USING THE IDEAS GRID

Once you have generated a number of tentative ideas, you'll need to find some way of focusing on those that will really work for you.

This idea originates with the 7×7 technique, developed by Carl Gregory. It helps if you can use blank postcards or small index cards. What works even better is to put a strip of Velcro on the back of each card and stick them up on a piece of material pinned to a wall or notice board.

1. Begin by writing out all the goals that seem important or attractive. Don't exclude anything because it seems unrealistic. Write them all on separate cards.

2. Combine ideas that are virtually the same. You might have both 'serving the community' and 'putting something back into society'.

3. Sort your draft goal cards into columns. Give each column a heading (e.g. financial, learning, personal).

4. Place the most important column on the left, the least important on the right.

5. You might want to apply a timescale, e.g. discard anything that you can't achieve within 2 years. So 'Find time to write my novel' might have to go on the back burner for a year or two. It's up to you.

6. Put the ideas in rank order within each column, with the most important at the top.

Now stand back and look at your results. Better still, go away and do something else for an hour, then come back and look. What you have is a draft *prioritized* grid, with the most important, critical or immediately relevant ideas in the top left-hand corner.

You can use the same technique to come up with ideas to solve a problem. For instance, if your problem is 'How can I change my career without going back to full-time study?' you can come up with a range of potential ideas and solutions, without self-criticism or feeling forced into a decision too soon. Reward yourself for off-the-wall ideas. Sort, re-sort, reflect.

'MUST DO' LIST

☑ Review Figure 4.2 and write down details of the times when you found 'flow'. What were you doing? What skills were you using?

☑ Learn how to think in different ways. Try a range of techniques for idea generation and problem solving (start by using them on everyday problems and then adapt them to career planning).

☑ Take dreams seriously, and see which ones will translate into goals. Write them down, somewhere, and tell someone you've done it.

☑ Write a Plan A for the next 12 months. Things to include: first steps on the journey, measurable goals, the critical steps you need to follow to make things happen (writing articles, going to conferences, talking to people, getting your CV rewritten, writing that book …).

Your Career Hot Buttons

This chapter looks at ways of:

▌ Identifying workplace turn-offs

▌ Measuring your career satisfaction

▌ Looking at money and motivation

▌ Piecing together your jigsaw job

▌ Discovering your career drivers

TURN-OFFS IN THE WORKPLACE

Go back to 'The good, the bad, and the just plain awful' in Chapter 2. Think about your hate list: the 10 things you would like to change most (about the work you do, or the way you are at work). Write them down.

You might find it helpful to categorize some of your dissatisfactions: physical work environment, location, people you work with, management style, status, recognition, people, tasks, variety, values of the organization, and so on. Make sure you have recorded all the things that demotivate or irritate you.

'I NEED THE MONEY'

Psychologists will tell you that money is rarely the primary motivator in changing jobs. People are often persuaded to take only a minor increase in salary, or even a pay cut, in order to get the 'right' job. Money only motivates in the short term: once you've got your fast car and the key to the executive washroom, the buzz fades pretty quickly. However, poor rewards can quickly demotivate, particularly where there is a sense of injustice. The thought 'I'm worth more than this' may begin from an awareness that you are underpaid.

How do you have any sense of what you are worth? I have known individuals being interviewed for £40,000 and £80,000 jobs in the same week, with little real difference in responsibility or complexity. Markets often do very odd things with salaries. Have you ever calculated what you really cost your employer, including overheads, and then calculated what value you add to the bottom line, whether actual in terms of profits or metaphorically in terms of your invisible contribution?

You ask what is the proper limit to a person's wealth?
First, having what is essential, and second, having what is enough.
                                                              Seneca

One interesting piece of research tells us a great deal about human psychology. When asked 'How much money do you need to feel that you have *enough*?', most people name a figure which is double their present income, whether they earn £15,000 or £150,000 a year. However, most careers books ask you to work out the minimum you need to pay all your bills and to eat. Unfortunately far too many people confuse this figure with what they are *worth*.

Write down a figure in answer to each question below.

WHAT DO YOU NEED TO EARN?

When you have added up all your monthly bills, travel, insurance, health and food costs:

What do you need to live on? | £ |

What would you need to earn to be relaxed about what you spend each month?'

What would be ENOUGH? | £ |

How do you value your skills, knowledge and commitment? What do other people like you earn in your chosen field? If you know the earnings range, what do you have to do to be in the top 25%?

What are you worth?

| £ |

On the basis that you have a greater chance of achieving something if you write it down:

What do you really want to be earning in 5 years' time?

| £ |

WHAT *REALLY* MOTIVATES YOU?

In order that people may be happy in their work, these three things are needed: They must be fit for it. They must not do too much of it. And they must have a sense of success in it.

John Ruskin

Recruiters will tell you that the first answer to that question is usually 'money'. The reason is that it's easy, convenient shorthand. In my interview training programmes I always try to get interviewers to probe to the next level. You may not be motivated by money at all, in fact. Throwing money at a problem does not make satisfied workers. Once money issues are resolved, deeper motivators kick in, such as being respected for what you know, seeing the job through to the finish, variety, making a difference, learning and work/life balance. If you want to check this out in more detail, try the Motivations Checklist in *Take Control of Your Career* or at www.johnleescareers.com.

What recruiters know is that everyone has Career Hot Buttons, but most of us are not good at identifying them (Exercise 5.2 will help). If you're asked why you want to leave a job, it's convenient to use shorthand: 'the job stinks', 'the money's rotten', 'it's the way they treat you'. We all have our convenient shorthand for the things that go wrong in life: work, car, house, marriage. To build on that experience it helps to ask 'What went wrong? What parts did I find uncomfortable or unhelpful?' and then actively seek the positive.

Knowing what you don't want is helpful, but only as a first step. This book is here to help you discover what you do want in your career, and to help you get it.

EXERCISE 5.1 – YOUR JIGSAW JOB

Here's a way of discovering what your ideal job looks like.

People find it difficult to describe their ideal job because it requires too big a commitment: a job title, a field of work, a potential decision. An easier way in is to use the jigsaw job technique.

You buy a jigsaw from a charity shop, but this is a jigsaw puzzle that comes in a plastic bag. You have no box, no picture, no title. You have no idea whether you have a picture of a cottage, a seascape or a kitten. So, in order to make the jigsaw you have to use other rules. You'll probably begin with the edges and the corners, but in the early stages of assembly you have to let go of the question 'what is this a picture of?'

Defining your 'jigsaw' job is like making a jigsaw without a box or the picture. You begin by making edges, corners and recognizable shapes. The analogy in career terms is that you forget about job titles and fields, and build the job up from the inside. Imagine you are in a really fulfilling job, but forget about what it says on your business card or on your door. Build the picture up from the edges, just thinking about each element in turn. Look at the example jigsaw job in Figure 5.1, and then fill in your picture using the same or similar headings.

My Jigsaw job will contain the following ingredients:	
Location, setting	Urban. Aesthetically pleasing. Flexible. Involves travel and meeting people
Hours	Generally Monday to Friday, but hours flexible
General details	A firm that's large enough to help me grow, small enough to support people
People	A role where I am mentored. Trusting, co-operative environment. Team working environment. Sharing ideas, thinking collectively
The way I manage	More a mentor than a supervisor
The way I am managed	I am given opportunities. My boss is direct, honest, sees my potential. Keeps me on the straight and narrow
Skills I use	Being the face of the organization. Liaising, explaining; translating complex ideas into straightforward terms. Communicating/influencing. Using creative and analytical thinking
Problems	Trying to help people with their problems. Completing work on time
Challenges	Competition: something to drive me. The job is testing/stretching. Learning about managing/leadership
Values expressed	Strong ethos. Clear sense of purpose/meaning
Likely/attractive outcomes include	Getting a team result. Bringing the best out of people. Delighting the client
The job will be rewarding because	I will be achieving something. It will be fun
How work contributes to life outside work	Comfortable lifestyle. Health. Well-being
Work will allow time and energy for me to do these things outside work	Spending time with family and friends. Enjoying the theatre and cultural events again

Figure 5.1   An example of a Jigsaw job

EXERCISE 5.2 – DISCOVER YOUR CAREER HOT BUTTONS

Table 5.1 provides a profile to check what motivates you in your career choices. First read the category title and questions. Against each category, circle a score on the scale of 1 to 10. Try to use the full scale rather than bunch all of your scores in the middle.

Table 5.1   Career Hot Buttons

1. Financial rewards

How important is the money, really? How much would you be re-energized if your salary increased by 10%? 20%? How long would that feeling last?

How diminished do you feel if the money is less than you are worth?

If you could do more of the great things about your job and fewer of the dull things, would you be just as happy with less money?

When you're at a party and listening to people talk about their jobs, do you always want to know how much they earn? Does it really matter?

Financial rewards are:

1	2	3	4	5	6	7	8	9	10
Unimportant			Moderately important				Very important		

2. Influence

Do you consciously enjoy exercising the skills of leadership, persuasion or motivation (high influence)?

How much control do you like to have over people, situations, problems?

You know how you like things done. Do you prefer to be in charge (high influence) or are you happy to follow a good leader (low influence)?

Do you like to have a say in change?

A high degree of influence is:

1	2	3	4	5	6	7	8	9	10
Unimportant			Moderately important				Very important		

3. Expert

How much do you like that feeling of being knowledgeable, skilled, an expert?

Are you happy knowing a lot about a focused area of knowledge?

Do you enjoy a reputation as a specialist (high expert) or a jack of all trades (low expert)?

Being an expert is:

1	2	3	4	5	6	7	8	9	10
Unimportant			Moderately important				Very Important		

4. Independence

Do you prefer a mentor to a supervisor?

Are you a self-starter? Do you like to set your own deadlines?

How much control do you like over how you spend your time?

Do you like to have control over what you do (high independence) or are you happy to accept intelligent supervision (mid to low independence)?

Independence in my work is:

1	2	3	4	5	6	7	8	9	10
Unimportant			Moderately important				Very important		

5. Relationships

How important are close relationships at work to you?

Are you more productive working in a team (high relationships) or quietly on your own (low relationships)?

How much do you enjoy getting to meet new people through work?

How important is it to you to trust and be trusted?

Relationships at work are:

1	2	3	4	5	6	7	8	9	10
Unimportant			Moderately important				Very important		

6. Security

How far do you need to feel you are financially secure?

That you have a nest egg, a safety barrier – a cushion against ill fortune (high security)?

How happy are you to take on risks of varying kinds (low security)?

How important is it to you that you know what you will be doing next week/next year?

Security in work is:

1	2	3	4	5	6	7	8	9	10
Unimportant			Moderately important				Very important		

7. Status

How much of you is contained in your reputation?

Do you seek recognition from your colleagues, your profession, your community (high status)?

Are you happy working in the background: as long as the job gets done, what matter who gets the credit (low status)?

How important is it to you to have a job title that reflects the level and impact of your job?

Status is:

1	2	3	4	5	6	7	8	9	10
Unimportant			Moderately important				Very important		

8. Meaning and purpose

How strongly do you feel about the value your work adds to your community, the world?

How aware are you of the damage your work might be doing to others, or to the environment?

Do you hear yourself saying that your work should be meaningful (high meaning)?

Are you happy to seek meaning outside your working life (low meaning, as far as work is concerned)?

My search for meaning through work is:

1	2	3	4	5	6	7	8	9	10
Unimportant			Moderately important				Very important		

9. Imagination

Are you good at discovering new ideas, new ways of doing things?

Do you prefer to let others come up with the good ideas while you do the detailed planning?

Do you prefer to follow a system or set of rules (low imagination)?

Or do you like to invent new solutions to problems (high imagination)?

Using imagination at work is:

1	2	3	4	5	6	7	8	9	10
Unimportant			Moderately important				Very important		

Your Total Scores

Career Hot Buttons	Total	Rank Order
1 Financial rewards		
2 Influence		
3 Expert		
4 Independence		
5 Relationships		
6 Security		
7 Status		
8 Meaning and purpose		
9 Imagination		

Write down your total scores, and then work out a rank order. If you have given equal scores to more than one button, balance one against the other. For example, if your scores for 2 (Influence) and 7 (Status) are the same, ask yourself 'Would

I prefer a job where my ability to influence or control others was *marginally* more important than my status?' If you have 3 or 4 equal, play 1 off against 2, then 3, then 4. It works, but if you have equal scores for some headings, no matter.

What are the implications? Match your top three career drivers against your present or most recent role. What is the degree of overlap? What is missing that you would like to add into your present job, or you will be actively seeking in your next post?

Occupational psychologist Stuart Robertson has been kind enough to build on my Career Hot Buttons when designing his very interesting **Career Motivation Indicator**. See www.sr-associates.com.

'MUST DO' LIST

Now you have identified your Career Hot Buttons, look back at what you discovered so far in this book:

- ☑ What really motivates you?

- ☑ What do you find unstimulating, unacceptable and demotivating?

- ☑ What might move you up the career satisfaction grid?

- ☑ How will you deal with 'Yes, but' and the limits it puts on your life?

- ☑ How far does your present job match your top three Career Hot Buttons?

Your House of Knowledge

This chapter helps you to:

▮ Tap your hidden knowledge

▮ Understand how your preferred interests provide huge clues about career satisfaction

▮ Make new connections between what you know, and what you can do

WHAT DO YOU KNOW?

Just as we all have hidden skills, we have concealed but vital areas of knowledge. What's powerful about your hidden knowledge is not just what you know, but why you know it. A certain amount of knowledge is inflicted upon us in school, but from the age of 14 or so we begin to make choices even about our academic subjects. All the subjects we read, learn and think about in our own time tell us a huge amount about our personality, aspirations and interests.

However, one point to beware: don't ignore the possibilities of new areas of knowledge you have yet to discover. One of the benefits of a demanding and eclectic education system is that it forces students to be exposed to subjects, materials and ideas that, at first sight, don't seem to be interesting at all. It's one of the reasons why exercises focusing on skills and knowledge don't tend to work with young people – they just haven't explored enough yet.

EXERCISE 6.1 – YOUR HOUSE OF KNOWLEDGE

This exercise helps you to identify, record, value and communicate the things you know about. It is also a vital step to help you to identify your areas of interest that may provide strong links into fields of work. What we choose to learn about is a vital part of who we are.

What do you know about? Ask that question of someone you meet on a train or in a pub, and most people talk first of all about the areas of knowledge most frequently used by their current job. They will often talk about their educational specialization. Therefore, 'My degree was in Spanish, but I'm an accountant now.' This is merely scratching the surface.

Look at the three-storey house in Table 6.1. It has a ground floor, first floor and second floor. It has an attic and a basement, and a garage at the side. Each level of that house represents something of what you know.

The exercise runs as follows. Like most exercises in this book, it works better if you have one or two people to ask you questions as you go along.

1. Begin with the **basement** of your house, the firm foundations provided by your home and school. The following questions will help:

   ▪ What did you learn from your parents? What was your favourite subject at school?

   ▪ What projects or activities engaged you outside the classroom?

   ▪ What was the first thing you wanted to read when you put aside your textbooks? What was that about?

Table 6.1   House of Knowledge

Attic
Subjects I pursue for pleasure
Self-taught courses

Second floor
Courses I have attended after
leaving full-time education

First floor
Work, including
on-the-job training

Ground floor
College/university/post-16
academic courses

Garage annexe
Interests held by
friends and
colleagues

Basement
Parents, home, school

- When were you so enthusiastic about a subject at school or college that you went off and found more to read in your own time?

2. Complete the list for the **ground, first** and **second floors**. Start with the straightforward information that appears in your CV, then try to remember the things you forgot you know about. Here are some prompts that have worked:

- Think about the training courses you attended that you got most out of. What were they about? What did you learn?

- What subjects led you to turning points in your life (that night school in pottery that made you change degree course ...)?

- What job have you enjoyed most? What did you learn from it?

- What subjects have you ever enjoyed training others in?

3. Move on now to your leisure pursuits, areas of personal interest and things you have taught yourself. This is your **attic**, the part of your brain where you store all that old junk you've forgotten you have, stuff you never thought you would find a use for. What areas of knowledge are hidden in those dusty trunks? Some prompts again:

- When your Sunday newspaper arrives, fat with different sections, which part do you turn to first? Which part second?

- When do you find yourself reading, talking or thinking about a subject and others have to shut you up? When do you find yourself so engrossed in an article or book that the time passes unnoticed?

- Think of a time when you have enjoyed learning about someone else's favourite subject or hobby. What was the subject?

- If you are an Internet user at home, which pages do you have bookmarked?

∎ If you were accidentally locked into a large bookshop for the weekend, in which section would you camp out? Once you got bored, where would you go next? And next? Write down the headings that would appear on the bookshelves.

∎ Given a free choice, what would you choose to talk about over a relaxed meal?

∎ If you could teach a workshop on any subject in the world, to any audience, and given unlimited preparation time, what would that subject be?

∎ If you received a bequest from an aged relative that would fund a return to full-time education, what would you study?

∎ If you could learn about any subject in the world, from any teacher, what would that subject be?

∎ If you won the lottery and didn't have to work, you'd spend a few months indulging yourself, and eventually you would get bored. What would you actually do to fill the time?

4. Last but not least, the **garage**. It's on an annexe at the side because it's about vicarious interests, living life through the eyes and minds of other people. Think about close friends whose interests you share. My friend Peter Maybank has a long-held interest in the First World War. I've joined him on battlefield trips to both Verdun and the Somme, and I realized through this experience how important the knowledge of others can be in shaping my own.

5. Look at your complete house. What have you missed out? It'll probably be things you consider 'trivial', such as cooking, homemaking or family history. If you enjoy it, include it.

It's important to remember what you are *really* interested in, and to remember all the things that you have chosen to know about. This tells you a great deal in terms of motivation and subject interests, and can lead you on to potential areas of work (moving from personal subjects in which you are interested into fields of work). This step is important because it's about recovering parts of your past which you undervalue, and interests that will give you energy and enthusiasm in the future.

KNOWING ABOUT AND PASSIONATE ABOUT – THE THINGS THAT WON'T LEAVE US ALONE

The attic of the House of Knowledge potentially reveals more about us than any other part of the building. This is where we store away the special projects, the things that call to us from time to time and just won't go away. When work feels like this we have our strongest sense of 'flow'. I had the chance to work with the Liverpool-based photographer Colin McPherson some time back and asked him in passing 'do you still enjoy taking photographs when you're not taking them for a living?'. 'Oh yes', he said, and showed me a card with one photograph on it, part of his long-term project photographing the last working salmon net fishermen on the east coast of Scotland.

'MUST DO' LIST

☑ Look at your completed house of knowledge. What activities in your past filled you with energy? Where is that energy today?

☑ Sit with someone else while they explore their own house of knowledge, and your partner's ideas will probably jog your memory.

☑ If you've caught yourself saying 'Ah, I *really* used to enjoy ...', then look at why you dropped the activity or interest. Is there a 'Yes, but' in there somewhere?

What do You Have to Offer?

This chapter helps you to:

▌ Map your hidden skills – the parts of your experience you took for granted

▌ Discover your potential, undiscovered, uncharted and motivated skills

▌ Find creative ways of looking at your toolkit

▌ Communicate your skill set to your colleagues, managers or potential employers

▌ Identify your achievements and express them as mini-narratives

▌ Compose brilliant presentation statements

My work is a game – a very serious game.

M. C. Escher

WHY IS LOOKING AT SKILLS SO IMPORTANT?

You use and observe skills every day, and you may think you're expert at cataloguing your own skills. Ask most people and they'll tell you 'it's obvious … it's just a matter of knowing what you are good at'. One of the greatest reasons people fail to achieve motivated careers is that they only ever see half the skills they actually possess. They only really know and develop 25% of those skills, and they only communicate a fraction.

If you want to make sure you never get a great career, one of the best strategies is never to reveal your full set of gifts. If you're determined to continue doing work that fails to stretch you or match your aspirations, that will do the trick.

Also, we are not simply what others see in us. It's too easy simply to accept the skill set that others describe – your friends see and affirm skills that they value; they don't always see the skills that really motivate you.

Example: Bill uses his computer every day, but his real interest is natural history. He gives time freely to his local school, which asks him to come in to fix computer problems or advise on software. If he is invited to do anything with the children, it usually involves explaining something about computers. He's great at it: probably the best person the school can find. But what he really wants to do is to talk to the kids about pond life.

First impression list

Divide a piece of paper into four boxes as in Table 7.1: Things, People, Information and Ideas.

Table 7.1 Skill categories

THINGS	PEOPLE
INFORMATION	IDEAS

Now write, in any of the four boxes, the skills you think you use most frequently. The following descriptions may help you to make sense of your results of performing an initial skills sort:

■ People who work mainly with **things** (and animals) – this includes engineers, machine operators, nature reserve wardens, vets, carpenters, car designers and gardeners.

▌ People who work mainly with **people** – this includes teachers, social workers, counsellors, trainers, salespeople and personnel officers.

▌ People who work mainly with **information** – this includes scientific researchers, librarians, auditors, archivists, editors, researchers and systems analysts.

▌ People who work mainly with **concepts and ideas** – this includes e-business pioneers, marketing professionals, artists, writers, campaigners and systems designers.

UNWRAP YOUR GIFTS

When love and skill work together, expect a masterpiece.

Charles Reade

The Hopi Indians believe that every person is born with a gift, and the purpose of our lives is to realize that gift in some tangible way. Unwrapping your gifts, exploring and celebrating the talents you have been given, is not just about work, or fun or duty. It's about discovering why you are here.

One of the ways we know that we live in an abundant universe is that we have a rich set of skills. We all have. If you're spiritually minded, you may have discovered that God, life or the universe, has sent you a particular set of *gifts*. It's useful to think of our skills as gifts, because it reminds us that what we do with those skills really matters – we have a responsibility to use them well.

Few of us see what a well-equipped skills toolbox we've been given. We use skills without recognizing or crediting them, and we fail to bring out our latent talents, blinking, into the light. You have been given a unique set of talents. Unique not because of one, primary, virtuoso skill that commends you to the world, but because of the way all your skills are uniquely combined in you. Unique because you are the only person with your skills, exercised through your personality, your history, your viewpoint. No one else can be you, in your particular situation in life. You can always find somebody who can employ a particular skill better than you, but they can't be *you*.

STEPS TO SKILL AWARENESS

The experience of helping career changers suggests to me that most of us have skills that we know well and are comfortable with, but there are huge areas of unmapped territory. You may find your own personal categories, but try these:

How many of your skills are:

Unconscious	Undiscovered
Undeveloped	Undervalued
Unsung	Unfulfilled
Unpolished?	

Unconscious skills

Unconscious skills are unseen skills, used so often that we hardly ever see them. Another way of describing them is 'wallpaper skills': they're ever-present, unnoticed, like wallpaper.

Example: Amy's great skill is making people feel better about themselves by talking to them. Others see her do it: it's oiling the wheels, increasing a sense of community. She does it so often she's unaware of it. She had never thought of it as a skill until a friend said, 'Do you know what you do most of the time? You're the cement between the bricks of our community.'

Key: You might become conscious of your 'wallpaper' skills when others point them out to you, which is fine if you have observant friends who notice that you're not aware of the thing you do best. A more active route to discovering unconscious skills is to measure what you do against your environment: how do I make a difference, regularly? Ask your friends

'What are my **wallpaper skills**?' (Then you'll need to explain the term!)

Undiscovered skills

Undiscovered skills are skills you use only occasionally, perhaps under pressure or in special moments. You often don't notice exercising these skills in the heat of the moment, or you don't claim ownership: things just happened. In an emergency, for example, there is often someone present who has great clarity of mind, organizing people, calling an ambulance and preventing panic.

Example: Maureen's great skill is untangling messy personal situations. She works quietly in the background, helping people to see things clearly, encouraging the parties to put anger aside and seek common ground. She never gets the opportunity to use these skills at work, so the opportunity only comes along very occasionally.

Key: Remember that sense of surprise – something changed because of your involvement. Why? What did you do? Ask yourself (or someone who saw you operating), not 'what happened?' but 'what did I do?' and 'how could I use this skill more often?'

Undeveloped skills

You possibly may see only the beginnings of undeveloped skills in yourself. Look for potential in clues, small seeds that may grow into something stunning.

Example: Norma has never been able to walk past a piece of fabric without touching it. She has a good eye for texture, colour and pattern, and for matching materials simply and cheaply to make a room look great. She has a knack of walking into a room and knowing how to make it look more welcoming, more 'together' by making a few simple changes. Last year her friend brought out these 'wallpaper' skills and found a set of undeveloped and marketable skills underneath – becoming a 'house doctor', helping other people to sell their homes quickly by reading the mind of the buyer and offering a series of low-cost, high-imagination solutions to make a home look great and sell quickly.

Key: Look at what you do, even in a small way; look at the component parts. Think about materials you love to work with, words you love to hear. Think of your skills as building blocks creating a structure you can't define yet. What can you build on? What can you learn more about? What skills can you use in a different way? Stretch yourself. Read books about subjects that seem of little interest. Go on courses on subjects you know nothing about. What do you do that might be a substitute for the real thing, e.g. buying art postcards when what you'd really like to do is fill your house with paintings?

Undervalued skills

Undervalued skills are skills you are aware of but you feel are of little value. You will hear yourself say 'I can do this, but who would be interested?' You enjoy using these skills, but you feel they have little currency, so you don't put any energy into cultivating or broadcasting them to the world.

One of the things I have always said while training recruiters is that there are no unmotivated people out there. There are those who show their motivation at work, and those who are motivated by exercising skills which they feel are of no value to employers. Often they will think of these as 'hobby skills'.

Example: Sue's hidden passion is ballroom dancing. She has never put it on a CV and keeps it quiet at work because she feels it is entirely irrelevant. One day she heard of a college lecturer who taught business skills through ballroom dancing.

Formal dancing teaches timing, responsiveness, leading and following, reading signals, anticipating change, paying attention to personal space. Sue realized that using these skills at work was what made her a brilliant PA. Now she proudly refers to ballroom dancing as one of her primary skills.

Key: These skills are often ones that you value highly, and you often use your personal time to find people who feel the same way about genealogy, antiques, fly fishing, whatever. If it's valuable to you, make it valuable to others. Look again at your undervalued skills – they are probably there somewhere in your working life in an unconscious or undeveloped state. Imagine what the world would be like without your contribution. Think of other places you might use your skills.

Sometimes these skills have become unappreciated by others.

Example: You're great at making a calm, tidy space in your home. But does anyone appreciate what you do? So you tidy, clean and dust with heaviness. How would you feel if your work was appreciated? If your job was to make a reception area look comfortable and welcoming – if your efforts made a difference? Are these skills you would love if someone else loved them, too?

Key: You should look in any skill you exercise for one essential component: passion. To find an inspired career there should be a metronome ticking inside you, repeating *These are the things I love to do and can do well. These are the things I'd love to do more of.*

If you are in demand for skills you don't enjoy using, either learn to love them or learn to say no. Tell people what you enjoy doing, and ask for opportunities so you can learn by doing. If you want a middle way, train someone else who will *really* love to do the things you can do well. Pass the skills on.

What if your skills are invisible to others, and that has changed the way you feel about them too? If you do something regularly, and do it well, ask yourself 'Do I need to do something else, something differently, or do these things somewhere where they will be appreciated?' Our skills, particularly those you are only just discovering, are tender shoots that need attention.

Unsung skills

Unsung skills are skills you have identified and valued, maybe skills you feel do have some relevance to the world, but you don't broadcast. You haven't yet discovered the right language to talk about them in a way that communicates them to someone who 'matters'. Job-changers often say 'I talk to my friends about this stuff all the time, but I don't know where to begin to tell an employer'.

These are often so-called 'soft' skills. This is a fine example of split thinking in the business world – hard skills are directly useful (selling, making, pushing, doing), soft skills are ten-a-penny and there in the background (imagining, feeling, training, sharing). We are often frightened that our 'soft' skills sound vague or prissy.

Example: Sally has held a number of voluntary positions, connected with school, church or Girl Guides. In the last 10 years she has acted as treasurer, leader, resource manager, transport co-ordinator, catering manager and team leader. She condenses this into a throwaway phrase on her CV: 'voluntary interests'.

It's true that employers often suspect that work done in a voluntary environment is pressure free, unconnected with the real world. Show them it isn't: give examples of working to deadlines, under pressure, to budget. Communicate how difficult it is to manage volunteers where you have to rely on persuasion and example rather than threat or coercion. Voluntary work often grows brilliant managers and self-starters.

Key: Look for those moments when you say 'things just happened ... it all came together at the last minute'. Who made it come together? If it was you, how did you do it? Finally, spend time discovering your skills; it's an inner journey worth taking because:

The minute you begin to do what you really want to do, it's really a different kind of life.

Buckminster Fuller

Unfulfilled skills

Your unfulfilled skills are the skills you dream about using, things you instinctively feel you might be good at if you only had the chance. Listen to those dreams calling you. I always wanted to ... paint watercolours, ride a horse, write my auto-biography, run a soup kitchen, build my own house ....

Don't confuse longing with fancy. You might dream about becoming a test pilot, but the test of longing is that the idea won't leave you alone until you do something about it. The crunch comes when you find an *activated desire* – in other words, a desire you can act upon. Want to be Prime Minister? Join a party, achieve some kind of elected office, take the first steps towards becoming an MP.

Watch particularly for tasks you dream about. I sailed as a boy and often dreamed about sailing again. At the age of 40, I did. It was everything I'd dreamed about, but better: because I had practised sailing so often in my head, I was actually better at it. I've heard this phenomenon called 'learning to ski in the summer, learning to swim in the winter'. All kinds of sports research has also confirmed that training by visualization is almost as good as the real thing. If that's true, then imagined skills are more powerful than you think.

Example: Steve knew he was a great ideas man. He worked in advertising as a copywriter and account executive, but what he did best was to get clients to really think about why they were advertising, and buy into a great campaign. His dream, half-formed at first, was to leave advertising and become a full-time motivational speaker and trainer. He kept at it, observing his own latent skills, picking up tips, gathering ideas, but his breakthrough came once he was sure of his potential, by telling others his dream. One client guaranteed him his first week's work should he ever go freelance. He took the chance, and has never looked back.

Key: Go for it! Nothing is as damaging as a ruthless policy of ignoring your unfulfilled dreams, either in terms of skills or in fields of work. Try things out. Test how activated your desires can become in stages, if that helps – try a job on a short-term basis. Work for nothing just to get the feel of it. Shadow someone doing the job to find out if it's what you'd really like to do. Take a short course rather than a 3-year degree.

Warning: These skills are most easily dampened by opposition or lack of support from others. People will try to steal or suppress your dreams. The strongest opposition can often come from your life partner, because you're threatening a complete change of lifestyle. Encourage your partner not to strangle your unfulfilled skills, and to give you space to experiment, but try to offer something back: time, explanation, feedback on what you are learning, maybe a deal ('If I do my nurse training for 2 years, then you can work fewer hours once I'm earning and restore that motorcycle you love so much but never have time to finish'). Teach your nearest and dearest how to be supportive, and reward them when they are – with affection, enthusiasm for their pet projects, breakfast in bed – whatever it takes.

While skills are still at the imagined stage, nourish them with care. Your brain is far better at producing skill barriers than your body. Find at least two fellow travellers who will not shoot your dream skills down in flames. Finding 'friends' who can tell you the downside is easy. They've tried it, they've been there. Brutal honesty is in oversupply in this world. Seek out positive support until your unfulfilled skills can breathe unassisted.

A new idea is delicate. It can be killed by a sneer or a yawn; it can be stabbed to death by a joke or worried to death by a frown on the right person's brow.

Charles Brower

Unpolished skills

Unpolished skills are rather like undeveloped skills, but with one important distinction: you are fully aware of these skills and value them, but you have settled for competence when you know you are capable of far more. The skill is stuck at a fixed level. It's not growing, and nor are you.

Example: Kate learned enough to get by in customer services: how to deal with different kinds of complaints, who to pass the calls on to, when to refer difficult calls to managers. She had learned the procedure inside out, but hated any change: new products, new support services. She had learned enough to describe her complaint-handling skills, but had failed to stretch herself, to see what she was really capable of, because she had never looked at the underlying master skill: keeping customers happy. Once she learned to develop that skill, to invent new ways of helping people, she began to grow and was promoted to supervisor.

Example: When you learn to swim, you begin by thinking of it as organized movement. Somewhere, you think, there's a special combination of movements that will keep me above the water and move me forward. The barely competent swimmer achieves that, and no more. *That'll do. I can swim.* Bill broke through that stage when he realized that swimming wasn't about movement or power, but a form of guided floating. With that idea in mind, he progressed to swimming several lengths. Then he discovered that it was also about timed breathing. Control the timing and breathing, and you can continue swimming just like you can continue walking. The first skill breakthrough will rarely be the last.

Key: Look for the underlying principle. Why are you doing this? What's the overall concept behind it? If your skill is selling, is the underlying principle profit, people, adding value, sharing a good idea ... ?

SKILL CLIPS

Think of your life as a movie. Your personal movie contains everything you've ever done, every moment when you've exercised any kind of skill.

When you want to communicate who you are and what you can do, you will tend to edit. You will show only short, quick scenes to your viewers. You edit your life like a movie editor, disposing of whole scenes, cutting, abbreviating.

The **skill clips exercise** sends you back to the cutting room floor, and fine-tunes your skills as a movie editor. When a distributor wants to persuade you to watch a movie, you get to see a trailer – the whole plot condensed into 30 seconds. That's your CV, if you like: a condensed, all-action version of you.

When a film critic wants to convey the character of a film, he will show you a film clip: an extract that shows a key scene, a special moment. In the movie of your life, what are the key moments? They may be the kind of events that you recorded in your photograph album. Go back and look through them. Do any of those occasions tell you anything about skills you have exercised in the past? (Incidentally, use your family photo album to remind you of areas of knowledge and interests – if you enjoy doing something, there's probably a photo of you doing it, somewhere.)

Fix on one event. Start with an occasion when you felt a great sense of success or achievement (maybe a 'flow' moment: see Figure 4.2). Picture your 'clip', and give it a title. Then ask yourself the following skill discovery questions:

What obstacles did I have to overcome?	What did I have to do to achieve this?
What was the task or challenge?	How did I work with others?
What planning did I need to do?	What was my best moment?
What skills did I see myself use?	How did I surprise myself or others?
What skills did others see me use?	What did I do personally?

Figure 7.1 shows you a skill clip example. Your skill clip begins with a title, like any good movie, but it also has a concise storyline – rather like the 'pitch' a writer has to make to a Hollywood studio to get an idea accepted.

Title: 'Top of the World'			
PITCH			
I've always been frightened of heights. I was pretty unfit. My work team challenged me to climb Cwm Clogwyn in Snowdonia.			
[Scenes] **Opening shot:** **The problem**	**First step**	**Main action**	**Ending**
Panic! Fear of failing. Sponsorship for a good cause convinced me to go ahead.	Weighing up the problem. Deciding what I needed to learn and practise.	Setting off – the real thing. Putting theory and training into practice. Scary!	I made it! Photograph at the summit. Elation.
Skills I used Recognizing my limitations. Overcoming fear.	**Skills I used** Learning from friends, practising on a climbing wall. Learning to climb and belay, understanding equipment. Risk management? Anticipating and measuring problems	**Skills I used** Working as a team, learning to rely on others. Responding (fast!) to instructions. Helping others to cope with their fear. Keeping people's spirits up with humour!	**Skills I used** Celebrating – enjoying what we had achieved as a team, and my special role in our success. Reflecting on what I had managed by overcoming fear and relying on my colleagues. Insight: new ways of working together.

Figure 7.1 Example skill clip

Home movie rules for editing and composing your skill clips

1. **Zoom in as tight as possible** – avoid long sequences. One day is good. One hour is better. Keep it concise. Like a movie clip, it's got to convey a lot in a short space of time.

2. **Use slow motion** – reveal the action as it happens by thinking about what you did and how you did it.

3. **Use a good screenplay** – does this scene convey a message about skills, about overcoming obstacles?

4. **Keep the star in shot** – make sure this scene is about the hero: you.

5. **Make sure the clip has a happy ending** – an achievement or a skill revelation.

Some prompts for your skill clips:

■ Think of times when you achieved something you are proud of. This doesn't need to be a work-related achievement. How did you do it? What difference did you make? Turn the event over in your mind until you see the skills, particularly those which are **unconscious** or **undeveloped**.

■ Now look at your achievements from your non-working life. Times in the past when you overcame the odds, did something that surprised yourself. Look in particular for skills that are **undervalued**.

■ Think about both **activities** and **accomplishments**.

■ Think about work related clips that demonstrate the full range of skills: things, people, information, concepts, etc.

■ Finally, what's your favourite skill?

Keep drawing up these skill clips, either alone or, even better, with a friend or fellow career developer. If you show a series of movie clips from the work of Alfred Hitchcock, you see similarities of style and content. After five or six skill clips you'll start to notice a pattern of skills, or a set of *master skills*, and you'll get a strong sense of what you are really good at *and* enjoy doing.

Express your achievements as mini-narratives

You can build on the skill clips exercise by learning how to remember each achievement as a mini-narrative. A good story is short and memorable, and has a clear topic. A good statement of your achievement has the same structure, as outlined in Figure 7.2, with a short explanation of the problem, a brief overview of what you did, and an indication of the outcome.

Story: Beginning	Middle	End
The problem My company needed to simplify its accounting system and save money.	**What I did** Identified, researched and introduced an off-site central accounting function.	**The outcome** 25% savings, and the new accounts centre came on line to budget and on deadline.

Figure 7.2   Achievement as mini-narrative

Using mini-narratives has great advantages. First of all, it's easier for you to remember good material to use at interview. You're providing yourself with a mental portfolio of useful evidence. Secondly, a well-constructed mini-narrative is easier to listen to and remember than a long, rambling tale. Thirdly, you don't have to think this stuff up during the interview. Trying to remember good examples in the interview room is hard work, because you have to apply several filters at once ('Will this sound interesting/relevant/impressive ... ?', 'Will it come out right?', 'Can I remember enough detail to answer supplementary questions?'). Having this information ready in the front of your head actually means that you can give more attention to using your interview radar, working out the *real* agenda (see Chapter 12 for more on interviewing).

Presentation statements

I am indebted to my colleague Bernard Pearce for the idea of presentation statements. At interview and when networking it's vital to give brief, upbeat responses to key questions. Being brief prevents you getting bogged down in possibly difficult details. Being upbeat focuses the listener on the positive, and interviewers in particular are far too good at remembering negatives. A presentation statement also allows you to communicate your skills and successes. This is something you work on a long time before you go anywhere near a decision maker.

Compose a brief statement, using your own words, to cover each of the difficult questions outlined below.

1. **Why do you want to change career?**
   Explain why you are looking for a new opportunity. Don't dwell on past problems or uncomfortable relationships, but discuss positive reasons for change.

2. **Where is your career going?**
   Describe the job you are looking for and why you find it exciting. Say why you believe you are suited to this kind of work, and stress how what you have to offer will help a prospective employer.

3. **'Tell us about yourself'**
   Compose a brief summary of who you are, what you do, and what skills and experience you have: encapsulate traits, skills and accomplishments to build a positive image in the mind of the listener.

4. **Summarize your career to date**
   Keep this to no more than 2–3 minutes, starting and ending with your present or last role and covering all the positive aspects of your experience that are particularly relevant for the position you are seeking.

5. **What are your strengths?**
   A concise overview of the skills and abilities that are likely to be of most interest to prospective employers. Remember that this is not a list of the job titles you have held or the companies you have worked for, but a shortlist of your main skills.

6. **What are your weaknesses?**
   This is always the toughest question. Avoid giving away any huge negatives. Usually it works if you admit to being something of a perfectionist or saying that you push yourself and

others too hard. Be prepared to talk about times when things didn't go so well at work, and talk about what you learned and what you would do differently next time.

7. **What are your main achievements?**
   Prepare more examples than you will actually need. Learn how to communicate achievements as mini-narratives (see above). State the ultimate benefits to the organization, including measurable results.

8. **What motivates you?**
   Be prepared to talk about what you have to offer rather than what you want to gain – talk about valuing the chance to use particular skills, opportunities to learn and grow or try out ideas. Stress the benefits to the organization.

9. **Why should we hire _you_?**
   How your skills, know-how and experience combine together in a unique way. This is your unique selling point (USP) – the reason(s) why you are the best person for the job.

10. **Why do you want to leave your present job?**
    Alternatively, this may be a question about why you left your last job. Whether you were pushed or decided to leave for your own reasons, keep your answer as short and upbeat as possible. If you were made redundant, a phrase such as 'the organization restructured and laid off a number of staff' usually works. Talk about what you want to do next as soon as possible. Avoid saying anything negative about a previous employer.

It usually takes more than three weeks to prepare a good impromptu speech.

Mark Twain

Skills plus: how employers see skills

How do recruiters measure skills? Most of the time, they rely on you: the claims you make in your CV and at interview, and the evidence you can find to back them up. Remember that employers see skills in terms of a context: how, where, when, why? Offer **skills plus**, your skills plus something – a problem, an attitude, an outcome. An employer is not interested in skills that are unattached to anything else: *I am a good communicator*. What kind of communication? What do you mean by good? Give me an example.

EXERCISE 7.1 – MOTIVATED SKILLS

What skills do you really enjoy using? Think about the time you have been so engrossed in a task that you lost all track of time, moments when you felt completely at home, yourself.

Look at skills you have identified and record them in a grid laid out like Table 7.1.

Skills in the darkest grey box are those you should be using and developing. If not, watch out for the consequences.

Table 7.1 Your motivated skills

	Skills I love using	Skills I quite enjoy using	Skills I don't enjoy using
Skills I perform well			
Skills I perform reasonably well but need to develop			
Skills I do not perform well			

EXERCISE 7.2 – SKILL CIRCLE

Take your identified top 12 skills and write them in a circle, like the 12 points of a clock, as in Figure 7.3.

Try combining skills. Ask yourself, 'When have I ever used these two skills together in an exciting or impressive way? What sort of work would benefit from a combination of these two skills?' You might, for example, combine 2, Managing people, and 7, Inventing solutions. This might mean: inventing new management systems, devising new ways of looking at management issues, such as giving people the tools to solve their own problems.

Combining 12, Challenging assumptions, with 6, Fund raising, might make you think about turning the whole idea of fund raising on its head. You might look at the question, 'how can we persuade more people to give us money?' and turn it around: 'how can we get people to persuade us to take their money?' Your fund-raising campaign may find a way of empowering people to select charities that exactly match their values.

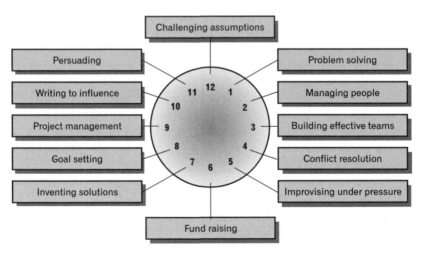

Figure 7.3   Skill circle

'MUST DO' LIST

☑ Find the best way for you of discovering your hidden skills. Enlist the help of a good listener, a patient friend or a professional careers counsellor.

☑ Look at the connections between your dreams, your interests and the skills you love using. There's a magic combination somewhere ...

☑ Try at least four skill clips. Write out the skills you discover. Look at the skills that keep coming up time and again – what are your **master skills** – in other words, the skills that are central to you as a person?

☑ Identify achievements for the different stages of your career.

☑ Plan, write down and rehearse your presentation statements.

FURTHER HELP TO IDENTIFY YOUR SKILLS AND ACHIEVEMENTS

It's virtually impossible to capture all your own skills. Most people need the help of a colleague or careers consultant. However, I have developed a set of skill cards that you can use on your own to give you a list of your **Top 10 Motivated Skills** and linked achievement stories. The cards come with a full set of instructions including several exercises you can use to help you understand and communicate your skills.

For full information about the **JLA Skill Cards** toolkit, designed to help both career changers and careers specialists, contact John Lees Associates (details are given on page iv, or visit www.johnleescareers.com).

For further tips on communicating your skills at interview, see *Job Interviews: Top Answers to Tough Questions* by John Lees and Matthew DeLuca (McGraw-Hill, 2008).

Finally, please note that all of the examples given in this chapter come from actual career clients. For further, detailed case studies of people who have read this book and moved on to new and exciting careers, see **Appendix 2**.

Who Are You?

This chapter helps you to:

▌ Explore your work and life values

▌ Understand what motivates you

▌ Gain insights into your personality

▌ Discover your different intelligences

Happiness is not having what you want, but wanting what you have.

Rabbi H. Schachtel

We looked in Chapter 2 at your *world view* and the way it affects your career decisions. Now we're going to explore some of the ways to help you to become more self-aware. The people who are most successful in their careers are:

▌ aware of who they are, and happy in that knowledge

▌ conscious of their motivated skills

▌ clear about the way these skills will be helpful to the world

▌ filled with something more than a surface confidence, but a deep-down confidence about what they have to offer.

Table 8.1 looks at a typical menu of options that a career might bring you, and looks at possible points of comfort and discomfort. Table 8.2 lists a range of typical **personal barriers**, and creative strategies to overcome them or get round them.

Table 8.1 Your personality in the workplace

	Comfort	**Discomfort**
Work role	The majority of the tasks you undertake and your overall role match your skills, temperament and areas of enthusiasm.	You find yourself doing too many things that seem meaningless, trivial or boring.
Work values	Your work relates closely to your wider life ambitions, your beliefs and your sense of purpose. You receive more than a short-term buzz. There is a sense that you are doing something important or meaningful, and your small part of the world is improved by the fact that you're doing it.	You feel that there is something missing. Maybe you're almost there, and what you need to do is to add other voluntary activities to your work portfolio. Or maybe there is something hollow about you: efficient on the outside, but empty in the middle?
Skills	You do things well and enjoy what you do. You have a sense of **flow**: time passes quickly and you are absorbed in your activity and proud of the results.	There is a significant mismatch between what you know, can do well and enjoy doing, and what your work role actually demands of you. You are doing some things extremely well, but discover that you really don't enjoy doing them.
Work context	Where and how you exercise your skills	A good benchmark of your discomfort is the

	matters. Do you prefer to work with people, things, information or ideas?	question *do you actually enjoy talking about your job*? This is not the same as the question *do you enjoy complaining about your job*?
Organization	Do you respond best to a small organization which offers variety and challenge or where you need to be self-reliant, or are you happier in the more defined structure of a larger organization?	Do you feel constrained by too small a firm, or by being an anonymous cog in a large concern? Perhaps you have struck the wrong balance between growth and security, between variety and structure.
Career drivers	See Chapter 5 for your **Career Hot Buttons** and compare your primary career drivers to what your job has to offer. How far is your present role in tune with your primary drivers?	If there's a mismatch, what would happen if you addressed your strongest scoring driver first? How would your present job change? What would be your next move?
Working conditions	Think about how your working life is affected by the following: location, travel, the kind of building you work in, what you can see from your office window, where you spend your lunch hour.	Now look at the same list in terms of the things that irritate and rob you of energy.
Growth, variety learning	Does your job keep feeding you? How are you different now from 12 months ago?	How do you begin to manage your career if you are in a job which does not offer growth or learning opportunities?

Career potential	Is your present role a useful stepping stone to the future? Do you have a clear plan for the next 5 years? Do you need one?	How would a recruiter see your present role: as a dead end, a side alley or a building block in your career?
Pace	Every job has its own sense of pace and speed. Does your organization make things happen quickly enough for you?	Are you being pushed at a speed which is faster than your natural or comfortable rate? How do you feel about leaving things half completed?
Change	Change, development and new opportunities fill you with energy.	You find change frightening or threatening.

DISCOVERING THE BEST YOU THERE IS

In the spirit of lateral thinking, I want to look at personality in terms of some recent thinking about the way businesses operate. In their exciting book *Sticky Wisdom*, Dave Allen, Matt Kingdon, Kris Murrin and Daz Rudkin recommend a number of specific creative behaviours often beginning with the question 'What if?'. Taking some of their thinking further, here are a few ways of starting a small revolution in 'You Plc'.

A fresh look

Look at Table 8.2 and ask what your working life would be if you assumed a completely different mindset for each box. To take a fresh look is to see things as if you just landed on the planet, or as if you were an inquisitive child: 'What does this do? Why do you do this?' It breaks you out of your habitual ways of thinking. Look at what normally energizes you in life.

If you obtain your energy from contact with others, then look at ways of finding your own company more enjoyable and productive. Just as you should get out of your normal physical environment from time to time, it helps to step outside your own personality.

Table 8.2 Personal barriers, and creative ways to overcome them

Lack of confidence	The key to getting an ideal job lies as much in your confidence as your skills or the state of the labour market. Seek out positive feedback and record it somewhere so you can retrieve it when you feel low. Resist every temptation to put yourself down.
Living up to your CV	You would be surprised to realize how many very senior people feel uncomfortable once they have prepared their CV. They feel that an employer will 'see through it'. They are worried about all those positive claims, and feel they are exaggerating. The reality is that employers, just like you, are good at latching on to negative pieces of information. So, don't give them the opportunity to do so. In your CV and at interview you should be the *best possible version of **you** that you can be*.
Fear of making mistakes	The world's greatest inventions are the result of mistakes. Mistakes are simply feedback on our performance. Winners make far more mistakes than losers – they get more feedback as they continue to try out more possibilities. The more timid mind stops after one mistake. Thomas Edison failed to invent the light bulb several thousand times before coming up with a version that worked. IBM chief Thomas Watson once said 'the way to succeed is to double your failure rate'.

Fear of rejection	Statistically you will be rejected more times than you are accepted. This is a fact of life, not a reflection of what you have to offer. The positive career changer looks at every interview, every discussion, as a learning opportunity. The most important question is 'what did I learn from this?' If you find yourself thinking 'all I learned was that people don't want me', then look again.
I don't know if I want the job	Research, and find out. Compare your 'I wish' list to the employer's 'We want' list. If it seems right, throw yourself at the opportunity with enthusiasm. If there are difficult decisions to make about moving house, or whatever, don't worry about them until the job offer is actually in your hand.
No achievements	Everybody has achievements. It's all relative. It is part of human nature to have goals and to overcome obstacles. The point is to recognize your achievements and to celebrate them, rather than assume they are of little worth and of no interest to others.
No clear direction	Not a problem, but a continuing opportunity. It simply means you have not yet finished exploring. Remember, though, that an employer is not interested in hearing about your areas of uncertainty. Do not use the job search process as a way of seeking answers to the questions you hold most deeply – all you will do is increase an employer's perceived risk.
Image	Find as many ways as you can to improve your own self-image (see the note on self-confidence above), but also learn to see how the world sees you. Ask your friends how they and others perceive you; most people find this feedback rather surprising.

Modesty	Many European cultures see the skills discovery process as boasting or self-aggrandizement. It's not. Boasting is when you come to the conclusion that you have something better than everyone else, and ram it down their throats. Discovering your true skills, talents and attributes is following a road to contentment, i.e. wanting what you have got. Objective self-criticism can be helpful and is sometimes painful, but should be a short-term burst of activity not a way of life. The human brain is finely attuned to living out negative messages, and we all gravitate towards our dominant thoughts. If you keep telling yourself 'I'll never be a manager' you will subconsciously use every ounce of energy to make sure that it becomes a self-fulfilling truth.
The shock of the new	It takes courage to make dramatic career changes, and courage to throw yourself into an entirely new job. Try to remember times in your past when you made similar leaps. How long, in fact, was your adjustment period? We are actually quite good at adjusting to new conditions. Even the most demanding and strange environment can become familiar and routine within a matter of months.
The expectation of others	Don't let other people live your career for you. Everyone does it – parents, teachers, friends and colleagues. They paint a picture of the future and you feel obliged to live it out. They often do so on scant information. You need two kinds of people to make these decisions properly: (a) skilled professionals who can help you to identify where your career is going, and (b) a core team of supporters who can positively encourage you to make it happen.

Lack of information	I talk to a great many people who try to imagine what new fields of work will be like. Imagination can be a helpful step in reaching a goal, but in an age full of information we can take solid steps towards finding out a great deal more. Talk to people who are currently doing the job. Find out what a job feels like from the inside.
Everyone I know is in the same boat	This particular mental block is common among school leavers and graduates. They effectively take a small sample of the population, which is the group of friends they socialize with. Every step forward or backward is judged in relation to that small peer group. There is often an interesting dynamic which holds back everyone except for the very strongest individuals. An antidote is to broaden your perception, increase your network, and try to find people who are living successful and balanced lives. Role models can be informative and inspiring.
Be careful what you ask for	One peculiarity of the brain is that we attract what we fear. If you see a small child carrying a glass of water and then say 'be careful you don't spill that', what happens? The child's focus goes from carrying to spilling. The drink is spilled. If you concentrate on the things you fear, you unconsciously put energy into a negative outcome. It sounds corny, but there really is power in positive thinking.
No goals	Set goals. Write them down. It makes a huge difference. If you can't set huge goals, then set small goals. Plan your week ahead: apply for a course, read a book, get an appointment with someone who works in marketing, increase your typing speed.

It's a dog eat dog world	*'Competition brings out the best in products and the worst in people.'* David Sarnoff
	Don't make the mistake of thinking you're in competition with everyone else. You're not. You're up against the requirements of a particular job and the needs of a particular employer. Co-operation is far more productive than competition. Pass on the lessons you learn about your own career explorations, and help others on their way. Beginning a network based on co-operation is the secret to a successful career.
Commitment	You need to think about what you really want. You need to think about the dreams that are simply dreams, and the dreams you can act upon.

You will also find it helpful to review your personal constraints using Exercise 2.1 (Chapter 2).

Protecting your ideas about your future

New ideas need 'greenhousing'; when we have new ideas sometimes the worst thing we can do is to share them with others and have them dismissed or trashed. Cultivate ideas quietly.

We all need rather more 'what if' thinking. Suspend judgement for a while; just let the idea ferment undisturbed, and stir the pot occasionally. Keep thinking up alternatives, possibilities, extensions.

Drains and radiators

In life there are two types of people: drains, who absorb the energy around them, and radiators, who push energy out. It pays to spend time with radiators when you are looking for career development energy. Radiators will say 'go for it'. Drains say 'that will never work'. Drains tell you to be 'realistic', which usually means doing next to nothing in the hope that something good will come along.

Being 'realistic'

An awful lot of career coaching goes on in everyday pub and coffee shop conversations, and often you'll hear someone talking about what they would just love to do in an ideal world. And, whether voiced or not, a presence stalks – the word 'realistic'. Because, held in opposition to that interesting 'ideal' world where work would feel like fun or a game, is a rather less exciting version – the real world. Time to be realistic, you'll be told (no matter what the economy is doing).

The word 'realistic' is the most dangerous in the career changer's vocabulary. This is *not* because I am encouraging people to try to shift into a fantasy world that doesn't exist. Good career coaching finds the right balance between inspiration and being entirely grounded in what is actually out there. A good career coach (see Chapter 15 for more tips) will be able to bring out the best in you *and* tell you how the market will react – to your CV, your interview performance, your 'pitch'.

Mistrusting the word 'realistic' doesn't mean avoiding the nitty gritty of getting a job. Why is it a dangerous word? Well, the question is this: *whose reality*? Many great ideas for career change are trampled by other people's 'Yes, but's', or by the jaundiced, narrow perspective of people who really do see the glass as half empty every time. What's real is this. If you get half a dozen seasoned recruitment consultants telling you that even with the best CV rewrite in the world you will never break into sector X, that's data. Everything else is just experiment. In short, keep pushing, keep finding out, and keep looking.

From imagination to reality

Captain Jean Luc Picard, second generation Star Trek Captain, executed his commands with three simple words: *make it so*. There comes a point where we have to make our ideas work. From 'what if' move on to 'how could I make this work … ?' Try thinking in terms of pilot schemes *and* experiments. In businesses these provide effective safety valves for introducing new ideas. We can apply the same thinking to our own careers by finding opportunities to try things out. One way is to extend yourself by going on courses, studying in your own time. Another is to take up some form of voluntary activity outside work in order to experiment with your career longings. Short-term or temporary employment can sometimes help to provide a useful 'laboratory' for your career plans. There is one useful principle here: 'don't think, just leap' – don't give up, just do it and see what happens.

Keeping the energy going

Companies find that habit, inertia and passivity effectively combine to make sure that new things do not happen. You can see the same forces operating in your own life. You need to recognize that your initial energy will start to fall away and inertia, or sometimes apathy, will take hold. Try to control and harness momentum by setting goals and planning for ways to re-energize yourself when you feel flat. If you get a brilliant idea for career investigation, anticipate that in some 3–4 weeks' time you will start to lose enthusiasm or feel a lack of confidence. Plan *now* to talk to someone positive at that critical time. Think of ways of committing yourself. Write goals down. Tell other people what commitments you have made so that they can help you to stick to them.

Learn how to think

Expand your range of thinking styles. Edward De Bono offers us **six thinking hats** which work well in the context of career planning, as described in Table 8.3.

Table 8.3   De Bono's six thinking hats applied to career transition

White hat	The information collector. What more facts do I need? Who else could I talk to?
Red hat	Emotions, feelings, intuition. What do I really feel about this? How far do I let these feelings affect my behaviour and my decision making? What gets in the way of change?
Black hat	Judgement, caution, conformity, truth. Will it work? Is it safe? How big is the risk?

(Warning: Black hat thinking can easily become 'Yes, but' thinking and suppress new ideas.) |
Green hat	Seeking alternatives, exploring, extending the art of the possible. How can I look at this differently? How can I generate new ideas for my career?
Yellow hat	Advantages, positive benefits. What would be the advantages? Why would it be good for me? How could I make it work?
Blue hat	The hat you use for thinking about thinking. The blue hat controls all the other hats, i.e. tells me 'isn't it time I used some yellow hat thinking, agenda setting here?'

Adapted from: Edward De Bono, *Six Thinking Hats*, Penguin Books, 2000.

Inventing your future

It takes bravery to take time out to think laterally and flexibly about the way your life is going. It takes even greater courage to tell other people about your discovery. It takes maximum courage to begin to put your discoveries into action. Those with higher self-esteem find it easy to adopt and explore new ideas, because those new ideas are not threatening their core selves. But don't make the mistake of trying to do it alone. Ask yourself this question: did you buy this book in order to avoid a conversation? In order to avoid talking to a career coach? In order to avoid networking? In order to avoid picking up the phone and finding out?

CELEBRATING OUR DIFFERENCES

He that is good with a hammer tends to think everything is a nail.
                                              Abraham Maslow

Understanding your personality can be a self-centred and
unproductive activity if it simply affirms an *I am what I am*
mentality. We're given clues about our personality types not in
order to fence ourselves off from the world, but in order to
build bridges.

Table 8.4 gives you a chance to record some broad indicators
about your personality. Think about the way you see yourself,
the way others see you, and the way you react under pressure.

After completing Table 8.4, ask someone who knows you well
to judge how far you have produced an accurate self-portrait.
Use this information to increase your level of awareness of the
way your personality operates in work.

Personality tests

There are a number of standard tests available. Tests such as
the Myers-Briggs Type Indicator (MBTI), the 16PF5 Questionnaire, or the Occupational Personality Questionnaire (OPQ)
should be conducted by a qualified practitioner. You should be
given a clear introduction to the nature of the test, how it is to
be used and who sees the results. You should be given objective, independent feedback.

There are also many other personality tests out there which are
not delivered by qualified practitioners. Hundreds of them are
online variants of dubious validity (making connections
between results and reality) and reliability (consistently
providing accurate information). Some recruiters use tests
which do not require a trained user. Any of these tests may
give you useful information and insights, but the results should
be treated with care. If you are unsure about feedback you
have received, arrange to be tested by someone qualified to
Level B by the British Psychological Society.

Table 8.4 Personality profile

Your understanding of yourself will help you to see where you will thrive in your next career. Where would you place yourself on each scale? (Avoid the mid-point, and please note that there are no 'right' answers – just prompts to give you an insight into the way your personality fits the world of work):

How would you describe yourself?

Confident								Cautious

Head in the clouds								Practical

Abstract								Concrete

Logical								Intuitive

Emotional								Analytical

Optimistic								Pessimistic

Open to change								Reluctant to change

Self-reliant								Need the approval of others

Emotionally vulnerable								Self-assured

Follower								Leader

Solo artist								Team player

Steady								Flexible

What energizes you?

People								Solitude

Activity								Calm

Thinking								Doing

Schedules								Improvisation

Groups or teams								One-to-one

The second problem with personality tests is that they give you a fairly clear picture of *how* you are, but there is no straightforward connection between personality type and the fields of work you might enjoy. When you are given your test results pay attention to where each of your scores fits on the overall scale. For example, no-one is entirely an extravert or an introvert. Secondly, reflect on your test results in terms of the way that others see you – how are you different from others? Finally, you will learn to 'read' other types around you and begin to see their preferences and the way they respond to situations. This gives you better strategies for communication and bridge-building with people who see the world very differently to you.

It's vital that you should not feel pigeon-holed by your results. Career explorers are vulnerable people, and will attach a great deal of significance to any job titles that are generated by career-related personality tests – you should certainly not conclude 'because I am an ESFJ, I should become a …'. In any occupational group you will find many personality types.

EMOTIONAL INTELLIGENCE

If you are all wrapped up in yourself, you are overdressed.

Kate Halverson

The concept of emotional intelligence has provided an important contribution to the understanding of the human mind. Where there was IQ, we now also have EQ. The ideas of EQ derive from the work of Yale psychologist Peter Salovey, who develops and expands on Gardner's ideas of interpersonal and intrapersonal intelligence (see Exercise 8.1 at the end of this chapter). One popularizer is Daniel Goleman, who suggests that people with well-developed emotional skills are 'more likely to be content and effective in their lives, mastering the habits of mind that foster their own productivity; people who cannot marshal some control over their emotional life fight inner battles that sabotage their ability for focused work and clear thought'.

There are five elements to an increased awareness of emotional intelligence:

1. **Knowing your emotions** – being able to monitor and describe a feeling as it happens.

2. **Managing emotions** – handling feelings as they arise, coping with our emotional reactions to setbacks and upsets.

3. **Motivating yourself** – marshalling emotions in the service of a personal goal.

4. **Recognizing emotions in others** – the fundamental people skill of empathy; being attuned to others' needs and the way they express them.

5. **Handling relationships** – managing and responding to emotions in others and displaying various forms of social competence, social skills, communication and leadership.

One of the most important features of any personality test is a measurement of your ability to cope with change, stress and working under pressure. Sometimes this is referred to as your emotional stability – an important factor when choosing your work culture.

Using your whole brain

You will often hear talk of 'left brain' and 'right brain' personality types. This is, of course, a metaphor; our brains are not ordered so simply. There are, however, some people who are more inclined to 'left' brain ways of thinking (organized, logical, systematic) and others who are more naturally 'right' brain thinkers (free-flowing, unstructured, abstract). In some personalities 'left' or 'right' may be dominant, but we are all a complex mix of both sides of our brain. The important thing is to discover your natural inclinations and build on them, and to learn how to communicate with those who see the world very differently.

EXERCISE 8.1 – DISCOVERING YOUR STRONGEST AREAS OF INTELLIGENCE

Professor Howard Gardner argues that intelligence is not a single faculty that can be accurately measured, for example by an IQ test. He believes we have several separate but related intellectual capacities, each of which deserves to be called an intelligence.

The following **inventory** helps you to discover your strongest intelligences, and matches them to your preferred style for developing ideas or managing problems.

Completing the Seven Intelligences Inventory

Please note carefully: the inventory which follows is not a psychometric test. The results are not intended to limit your occupational choices or give you a distinctive personality 'type'. Its aim is to add to your understanding of the way you see the world, and suggest further areas of exploration in terms of:

▌ the way you learn

▌ the way you interact with others

▌ the way you respond to different personality types, e.g. in a team

▌ the skills you enjoy using

▌ interests that might develop your 'weaker' intelligences

▌ fields of work where you might develop your primary intelligences.

Under each of the seven headings is a list of characteristics. Tick any sentence that describes what you are like most of the time. There are no right or wrong answers – if in doubt, put a tick. Then give yourself a score between 1 and 5 after reading the longer description of each intelligence.

Add up your total score out of 15 for each category, and transfer your scores to the final panel. At the end of the inventory write down your three strongest intelligences.

	Linguistic intelligence	
		TICK
1	I enjoy language and word games	
2	I enjoy crosswords or other word games	
3	I like telling stories or jokes	
4	I enjoy reading for pleasure	
5	I enjoy choosing the right word	
6	I like listening to spoken word programmes	
7	I enjoy intelligent debates	
8	I hear words in my head before I speak or write	
9	I can often remember exactly what was said to me	
10	I rehearse things verbally in my head	
Total number of ticks/10	**Score** ⇨⇨⇨ ☐	

Linguistic people enjoy reading and writing, love word games, and are responsive to the spoken or written word, and the richness of language. They often have a good memory for names. They possess a wide vocabulary and speak and/or write fluently.

Give yourself a score between 1 and 5 in terms of how well this paragraph describes you

Not me at all   Spot on

    1   2   3   4   5   **Score**   ⇨⇨⇨ ☐

Linguistic intelligence   **Total combined score/15**   ⇨⇨⇨ ☐

Logical–mathematical intelligence

		TICK
1	I am good at mental arithmetic	
2	I enjoy games or puzzles which require logical thinking	
3	I enjoyed maths and/or science in school	
4	I enjoy practical experiments	
5	I enjoy strategy games like chess	
6	I like things to be clear and well organized	
7	I think things through logically	
8	I am interested in new developments in science	
9	I like to have prioritized lists	
10	I believe that most things have rational explanations	

Total number of ticks/10   **Score**   ⇨ ⇨ ⇨ ☐

Logical–mathematical people respond well to patterns and structures, and prefer to do things in a sequential order. They organize experiments to test theories, and enjoy opportunities to solve problems. They reason things out logically and clearly.

Give yourself a score between 1 and 5 in terms of how well this paragraph describes you

Not me at all   Spot on

    1   2   3   4   5   **Score**   ⇨ ⇨ ⇨ ☐

Logical–mathematical intelligence   **Total combined score/15**   ⇨ ⇨ ⇨ ☐

	Visual–spatial intelligence	
		TICK
1	I can interpret plans or diagrams easily	
2	I quickly understand symbols on signs, instrument panels and equipment	
3	I enjoy cartoons	
4	I like to draw, sketch or doodle	
5	I enjoy photography	
6	I have a good sense of direction	
7	I prefer books with illustrations and diagrams	
8	I am good at giving road directions	
9	I am good at reading maps	
10	I feel strongly about the layout and 'look' of a document	

Total number of ticks/10   **Score** ⇨⇨⇨ ☐

Visual–spatial people tend to think in images and pictures. They enjoy visual puzzles and mazes, and tend to organize ideas visually in their heads, drawing maps or networks to connect ideas.

Give yourself a score between 1 and 5 in terms of how well this paragraph describes you

Not me at all   Spot on

1   2   3   4   5   **Score** ⇨⇨⇨ ☐

Visual–spatial intelligence   **Total combined score/15** ⇨⇨⇨ ☐

	Bodily–kinaesthetic intelligence	
		TICK
1	I would rather drive than be a passenger	
2	I prefer it when my hands are occupied with something practical	
3	I find it difficult to sit still and relax for long periods	
4	I am well co-ordinated physically	
5	I am good at building or repairing things	
6	I enjoy hobbies which have a physical result like carpentry, wood carving, knitting, model building, gardening	
7	I enjoy physical sport or exercise	
8	I like to spend my free time outdoors	
9	I enjoy human touch and use expressive body language	
10	I would rather play than watch	

Total number of ticks/10   **Score**   ⇨ ⇨ ⇨ ☐

Bodily–kinaesthetic people like to interact with the world physically. They have an ability to control their bodies and handle objects skilfully. They respond best to work that is physically active, 'hands-on' and practical. They often enjoy sports and the outdoor life.

Give yourself a score between 1 and 5 in terms of how well this paragraph describes you

Not me at all   Spot on

      1   2   3   4   5   **Score**   ⇨ ⇨ ⇨ ☐

Bodily–kinaesthetic intelligence   **Total combined score/15**   ⇨ ⇨ ⇨ ☐

Musical intelligence		TICK
1	I have a good 'ear' for music	
2	I can hold a note	
3	I sing or play a musical instrument	
4	I often remember tunes in my head	
5	I would rather listen to music on the radio than discussions	
6	I can follow a musical score	
7	I have a good sense of rhythm	
8	Music speaks to me emotionally	
9	I am very aware of an 'off' note or an instrument which is out of tune	
10	I enjoy rhymes, poetry, and limericks	

Total number of ticks/10   **Score**   ⇨ ⇨ ⇨ ☐

Musical people respond well to sound, music and rhythm. They often have a talent to interpret or produce music. They will often find it helpful or soothing to listen to music while studying or reading. Music will often 'speak' to them in terms of colours, emotions or themes, even when there are no lyrics.

Give yourself a score between 1 and 5 in terms of how well this paragraph describes you

Not me at all   Spot on

  1   2   3   4   5   **Score**   ⇨ ⇨ ⇨ ☐

Musical intelligence   **Total combined score/15**   ⇨ ⇨ ⇨ ☐

	Interpersonal intelligence	TICK
1	I would rather be in company than on my own	
2	I'm a good listener	
3	I prefer group sports like football or badminton to solo sports like swimming or running	
4	I generally talk about my problems with my friends	
5	I enjoy parties and other social events	
6	If I learn a skill I am happy to teach it to someone else	
7	I can pick up on the moods of other people	
8	I can express an idea best by talking about it	
9	I have a number of close friendships	
10	I am often called on to manage teams or organize social activities	

Total number of ticks/10   **Score**   ⇨ ⇨ ⇨ ☐

Interpersonal people are interested in others around them, are good listeners and communicators. They prefer to be in company, and like to share with others. They are naturally inclined towards teaching, caring or nurturing roles.

Give yourself a score between 1 and 5 in terms of how well this paragraph describes you

Not me at all   Spot on

     1   2   3   4   5   **Score**   ⇨ ⇨ ⇨ ☐

Interpersonal intelligence   **Total combined score/15**   ⇨ ⇨ ⇨ ☐

Intrapersonal intelligence		
		TICK
1	I enjoy my own company	
2	Learning and personal development are important to me	
3	I have some strong opinions	
4	Spending time alone reflecting is important to me	
5	I have a strong sense of intuition	
6	I enjoy a quiet space in order to meditate and reflect	
7	I keep a journal that records my thoughts and feelings	
8	I have a strong sense of independence	
9	I normally solve my own problems	
10	I would probably enjoy being my own boss	

Total number of ticks/10   **Score**   ⇨ ⇨ ⇨ ☐

Intrapersonal people value time spent alone and are very aware of their own personality, strengths and weaknesses. They tend to solve problems alone. They are often highly independent and self-motivated. They value the inner self, personal development, and spirituality. They may be entrepreneurs or interested in becoming self-employed.

Give yourself a score between 1 and 5 in terms of how well this paragraph describes you

Not me at all   Spot on

    1   2   3   4   5   **Score**   ⇨ ⇨ ⇨ ☐

Intrapersonal intelligence   **Total combined score/15** ⇨ ⇨ ⇨ ☐

Primary intelligences	Your total
1. Linguistic intelligence Using and loving language, whether written or spoken	
2. Logical–mathematical intelligence Using or interpreting numbers, data, facts, sequences, scientific research	
3. Visual–spatial intelligence Seeing things in pictures or images, map-reading, making 3D models	
4. Bodily–kinaesthetic intelligence (sometimes known as 'physical intelligence') – the ability to control one's body and handle objects skilfully	
5. Musical intelligence Having an 'ear' for music, a talent to interpret or produce music	
6. Interpersonal intelligence Communicating with and responding to other people	
7. Intrapersonal intelligence Valuing personal growth, independence, reflection, meditation – the inner world	

Your three strongest intelligences

Interpreting your primary intelligences

What do the results mean? First of all, they should make you look again at the way you respond to people whose intelligences are very different from your own (it can be very difficult, for example, for visual–spatial people to understand what those with high linguistic intelligence are explaining in such a long-winded way. They will say 'just draw me a diagram!')

How can the results help your career choice?

It will be rare that you will see a direct correlation between one strong intelligence and one occupation, e.g. 'I should be a mathematician!' Your intelligences combine with your preferred areas of knowledge, your motivational skills, your upbringing and your personality.

Here are some pointers in relation to strong scores. In every case what you may be spotting is an opportunity to expand your natural intelligences.

Linguistic intelligence – Does your work give you opportunities to express yourself clearly in writing or in speech? Where can your organization improve its communication? How can you adapt messages so that they are better perceived by those who have strong intelligences in other areas?

Logical–mathematical intelligence – Your preferences lie with numbers, statistics, data or scientific investigation. How far is this intelligence being stretched? Do you have difficulty communicating what you see in numbers to others?

Visual–spatial intelligence – Where in your job is this intelligence used? Can you learn how to use software to design slides and presentations? Can you make signs or posters?

Bodily–kinaesthetic intelligence – What happens if your work is entirely intellectual and desk-bound? Can you translate your work into another context (e.g. move from management training to outward-bound leadership training)?

Musical intelligence – Can your musical intelligence be used in any way other than a career in music, e.g. in sounds, jingles, rhymes (perhaps in advertising copy or rhymes to help people to learn and remember things – 'an apple a day ...').

Interpersonal intelligence – Your skills in 'handling' people and relationships are much in demand in the modern workplace. Which aspects of interpersonal intelligence are strongest for you, and which need nurturing?

Intrapersonal intelligence – Do you take your inner world seriously enough, and apply reflection to your work? Some managers consciously set aside thinking time when they can reflect. Don't always take work with you on the train. Sit and think. Advice to this group might be 'Don't do something, just sit there ...'.

'MUST DO' LIST

Questions to help you to reflect on your personality and working style:

☑ What brings you to life? When or where do you become *energized*? What has a deadening effect on you?

☑ How far do you really understand your own personality? Can you define the kind of work roles where you will be most effective *and* comfortable?

☑ What barriers to career success have been caused by your problems reading people, and getting them to understand your 'take' on life?

☑ How well can you anticipate the results of any personality profiles that will be used by selectors? Are you ready to answer questions about your strengths and weaknesses?

CAREER AND PERSONALITY TESTS

Quintax is a highly reliable but also very user-friendly personality test that gives useful feedback on thinking styles, team fit and areas for development. Visit the website www.sr-associates.com or telephone Stuart Robertson & Associates on 01618 773277.

Career Horizons is also highly recommended. This software suite provides information about your skills, learning style, and personal career goals. Visit the website www.careerhorizons.net or telephone Stuart Mitchell & Company Ltd on 01483 423943.

What is the Right Field of Work for You?

This chapter helps you to:

■ Discover the importance of field in career choice

■ Find a range of ways of discovering fields

■ Identify subjects, fields and areas for investigation

■ Use lateral thinking to help you to identify new fields of work

Work is much more fun than fun.

Noel Coward

FIELDS OF WORK

What is a field?

A **field** is a way of categorizing work. Fields are sometimes known as 'sectors' or 'domains'. Imagine an office full of filing cabinets. There is a file for every job you can imagine. If you had to organize that information in some way, you would group jobs together into separate headings. These we call fields or sectors.

Some fields are huge. Think of medicine – a large and very general field. Within that large 'job family' are several smaller fields, including nursing. But even if you choose nursing, you will soon have to decide whether you want to be a general hospital nurse, a nurse dealing with mental health, children or old people, an operating theatre nurse, or perhaps a community nurse, a nurse in a health centre, or an occupational nurse in a factory environment. Qualified nurses can also find themselves acting as teachers, counsellors, managers or expert witnesses. So within any field there is a huge number of occupations.

WHY FIELDS ARE POWERFUL

Many careers counsellors believe that your choice of occupational field is one of the most powerful factors in taking you to an inspired career.

Let's take another job title: teacher. We think we know what a teacher does. But this role can appear in a number of fields in interestingly different ways, for example:

- a teacher of sign language to parents of deaf children
- an education officer interpreting a nature reserve to the public
- a gallery officer making art and sculpture exciting for children
- a salesperson demonstrating the potential of new software
- a business consultant specializing in team building
- a motor mechanic supervising apprentices.

Fields and funnels

The essential truth is that human society needs to find some way of categorizing everything, and this includes ideas and activities. This begins at school. You didn't have classes titled thinking, speaking, imagination or wisdom. Actually, you might have attended such classes if renaissance ideas about education had continued to the present day. In the Victorian age educators reclassified what was taught into much narrower boxes (and at the same time invented new subjects, including English and physics). The subjects you are taught in the class-room lead naturally to educational and career decisions. We have all got used to putting knowledge into separate boxes: music, history, French, chemistry. These boxes shape the way you imagine your adult life will be, following a simple construct: 'I'm good at science so I should be a scientist.'

This process of 'educational funnelling' is the basis of much of our early careers advice. You see a box with a label on it that looks attractive. The label shows somebody doing things which look rather like activities you have enjoyed at school, whether this involves grooming animals or handling test-tubes. You are attracted towards that box because of the idea that this field will be like something you have already enjoyed or shown some talent in before.

This approach falls down in a number of ways. Firstly, your secondary education narrowed your studies down to no more than about a dozen subjects, but there are literally thousands of fields of knowledge and work out there. Anyone working with school or university leavers needs to explore this thinking carefully: there are few people practising 'pure' geography, history or mathematics in the world.

Fields and motivation

Find a job you like and you add five days to every week.

H. Jackson Browne

It's easy to choose a field that seems 'safe'. At times of crisis you will tend to gravitate towards fields where you can operate inside protective boundaries – your comfort zone. It's common among career changers to hear people say 'I would really like to work in a field which inspires me, but I will find it much easier to get a job in the field I have been working in for the last 20 years'.

Talk to people who love the field they are working in. You will hear in their voices enthusiasm, love of detail, a willingness to share what they know with others, and a wish to encourage others to follow the path they have taken. Once you find a field that gives you the same 'buzz', you will approach both your job search and the work you do with a far more positive spirit. The spin-offs, both for yourself and for any organization which employs you, are important:

■ You will be more enthusiastic at interviews – and employers love enthusiasm.

■ You will retain what you learn and enthusiastically pass it on to colleagues.

■ Your love of your work will communicate itself to clients and increase their loyalty.

■ You will find it far easier to fit into an organization where others share your passion.

■ Efficiency and productivity will come naturally to you.

■ You will be forever interested in new ideas, new connections and increasing your learning.

Limitations of fields 1 – Choosing too narrow a range

The problem with looking at fields is that they are just ideas in boxes. They can be extremely helpful and practical in terms of a job search. You may end up identifying between 5 and 15 organizations in your local area in suitably attractive fields, and you can begin a highly active and targeted programme of making speculative approaches and networking.

However, fields can often be very restrictive. You may choose fields that are obvious and safe. You may focus only on one area of interest and fail to ask 'What parts of me will *not* be developed if I work in this field?'

Let's say your interest is forestry. You like working outdoors in the wild woods. You go through the training which adds to your depth of background knowledge about forestry and conservation. You get a job. You find yourself dealing with peripheral problems such as record keeping, litter or car parks. You find that less and less of your knowledge and enthusiasm is being tapped, and you are increasingly learning about regulations, funding and government initiatives. Possible career crisis. You find yourself saying 'I came into forestry because I love conservation and wildlife, but I've become a bureaucrat'.

I hear the same story almost every week from people in teaching, personnel, nursing, travel, university lecturing and ministry, among a wide range of fields. 'I was attracted by the box called Nursing', they say, 'and I liked what it said on the label: caring for people, being there for patients and relatives. What am I now? A form filler.'

Limitations of fields 2 – Not knowing what's out there

I tell people that career choice is like trying to plan a journey using a map that is full of blank spaces. Field discovery helps to fill in those blanks.

If you can't find a field that suits you, you may have to find a new angle. Work is changing so rapidly that new fields are being created all the time. Maybe you'll dream up an entirely new field. Before Galileo there really wasn't a field you could describe as experimental physics. Before Freud there wasn't a field called psychoanalysis.

You can only begin to really know what's out there by being fascinated by what's out there. It can't be just an exercise. One characteristic about people who have made huge, brave career changes is that they became excited about what they didn't know – and started to do something about the gap in their knowledge. Chapter 10, designed to help you if you sense that you want to do something completely different, will also point to the importance of active exploration.

The best way to predict the future is to invent it.

Alan Kay

Limitations of fields 3 – Starting with the wrong idea

A huge amount of the information we hold about fields of work comes, at best, secondhand. We rely on out of date information from family, colleagues and friends. The problem is that most of this information is filtered and interpreted by someone else, and probably out of date. It doesn't give you an overview of the job.

The second problem with this kind of prompt is that the information is weighted. When people describe jobs to you they attach value tags (safe/risky, dull/exciting, boring/cutting edge, fixed/changing). Sometimes this information is entirely on the button, providing you with really important clues about what work is actually like. At least 50% of the time, however, it's out of date, subjective, or just plain wrong.

The first principle is to start with your own impulse, not with someone else's idea of what a job is like. Find out for yourself. Don't rely on the slanted, possibly jaded views of retired professionals, recruiters or friends.

And remember that *the* great question to ask about any job is 'What do you do most of the time in this job?'

Limitations of fields 4 – Moving on from subjects to fields to choices

A common place where my clients get stuck is that they identify subject areas that interest and inspire them, but they can't make a connection between a subject of interest (e.g. gardening) and a field of work. They succumb too quickly to either/or thinking: fields are for work or pleasure. You will hear some career counsellors say things like 'maybe you should follow this interest in your spare time'. Even more worrying is the idea 'If I do what I love for a living then I might get sick of it … better to have an ordinary job and do what I love in my own time'. All this can be a great way of keeping work separate from 'life', in other words, a new excuse for avoiding enjoyable and interesting work.

If you can't see how you can move from subjects you love to potential fields of work, you need to do some work on ways of making connections. Exercise 9.1 shows you how.

WAYS OF IDENTIFYING FIELDS

Where do I begin? Identifying fields that will interest and inspire you

Begin with yourself. Look back at your House of Knowledge in Chapter 6. What subjects, topics and themes energize you? What do you love learning or talking about? What do you want to know more about?

Prompts to thinking about fields

Use this tried and tested prompting sequence to identify possible fields of work:

Stage 1 – Remembering

1. Dream jobs you had as a child.

2. The most enjoyable topics you have studied.

3. Any of the fields you've worked in, or near.

4. Fields where your friends, family or contacts work.

5. Jobs done by friends which you find fascinating.

6. Jobs that attracted you in the paper, even if you never applied for them.

7. Particular assignments or projects you enjoyed.

Stage 2 – Three great days at work

8. Think about a time when you had a great day at work. The sort of day where everything went well and you went home energized. Write down what you were doing, what you enjoyed and what you achieved.

9. Do the same thing for two other memorable days.

Stage 3 – Imagining

10. What jobs have you ever imagined doing?

11. If you could try someone else's job for a day, what would it be?

12. If you could do any job in the world for a week and still receive your normal salary, what jobs would you try?

13. Who are your role models or champions, and what fields are they in?

14. If you won a million pounds and you didn't need to work, what activity would you happily do for nothing?

Analysing job themes

Starting from the inside means putting together a working recipe for the kind of job that will work for you. One simple index of whether the job will work well for you is to think about the Job Themes that appeal to you most strongly– see Table 9.1.

Table 9.1 Job Themes

Job Theme	Description	How strong is your interest in doing this in your next job? 3=Strong interest 2=Mild interest 1=Weak interest 0=No interest at all
Working with and for **PEOPLE**	Your ideal work is *mainly* about working with people, e.g. helping, caring, nursing, nurturing, developing, healing, coaching, mentoring, or teaching ...	
Working with **INFORMATION**	Your ideal work is *mainly* about working with information, e.g. analysing, cataloguing, gathering, planning, managing projects, researching, tracking down information, working with numbers or accounts, making the most of computers ...	
Working with **REAL OBJECTS**	Your ideal work is *mainly* about working with the physical world, e.g. building, shaping, cooking, craft, DIY, working with animals, plants, working outdoors, machines, vehicles, sports, physical fitness, hands-on therapies ...	

Working to **INFLUENCE**	Your ideal work is *mainly* about working through other people and will involve: leadership, management, changing organizations, setting up a new business or department, inventing, re-organizing, shaping teams, driving others, influencing, persuading, motivating, selling, getting results ...
Working with **IMAGINATION**	Your ideal work is *mainly* about working with ideas or creative activity, e.g. being active in the arts, performing, creative writing, lateral thinking, business creativity, adapting ideas, coming up with new ideas, challenging assumptions ...
Working with **SYSTEMS**	Your ideal work is *mainly* about working within systems, e.g. book-keeping, quality control, continuous improvement, legal frameworks, procedures, health and safety ...

Look at your top three Job Themes from Table 9.1. The answer to the way your career puzzle comes together is clearest here. How is your career a unique interaction between these three? How can you make sure that your work feeds all three? For example, if your top three Job Themes in order are **Imagination, People** and **Real Objects**, you'll want to ensure that your work allows you a high degree of creativity generated by teams of people, the chance to invent new rules from time to time, but you'll be happiest working where you achieve results you can see and feel. Remember, your Job Theme combination is a combination unique to you, because it also draws upon your knowledge, values and experience.

Try out your Job Theme combination as a working recipe for your ideal job. Add information about your skills to the mix. Combine this information to the master sheet at Table 16.1. Using the master sheet helps you bring all your career ideas together into one place.

It's important to keep checking your results. The more you learn from this book about your ideal job, the more you need to ask questions of other people: a question along the lines of *what does this combination of information suggest to you*?

If I could do anything at all ...

If you're discussing career choices with a friend, a common question is 'What would you do if you could do anything?' Another variation, which I prefer, is 'what would you do if all jobs paid the same?' The interesting thing is that having taken status and money out of the picture you can focus very simply on that key question: *what would I be doing most of the time?*

Another common prompt (used in Chapter 6) is 'what would you do if you won the lottery?' Those people who have won millions on the National Lottery in fact do seem to demonstrate an interesting pattern of behaviour. After playing with the money for a year or two, buying houses, holidays and cars to match their acquired lifestyle, they then tend to get bored and look for something to do. For some this means setting up or investing in a business, a charitable foundation or something similar. One man even went back to his job as a staff trainer for the McDonald restaurant chain. So the real question is 'if you won the lottery, what would you do 2 years later when you were bored and could do anything you wanted?'

Resources

Finally (and don't ignore this one because it seems too obvious), use books about occupations and career choice as ways to add to your list of possible fields (see the website recommendations in Appendix 3). An alternative method is to go through the Yellow Pages for your nearest city and mark any field that interests you. Look at books about unusual occupations like *Offbeat Careers*. Many trade bodies publish guides giving entry requirements, training details and prospects. Read the careers pages of general newspapers: sections on graduate careers often contain career tips and company information useful to the full range of job seekers.

Confidence

Notice that moment of hesitation before you write down the name of a field. Look at what's going on through your head. *I'll never get into this field of work. I don't have the training. I don't know enough.* In those moments remember this: President Abraham Lincoln carried with him everywhere a newspaper clipping stating that he was a great leader.

Pushing field alternatives

The ability to push for alternatives is a powerful thinking skill for all aspects of life. The natural tendency of the mind is to move towards certainty and security. We often shun alternatives. A training colleague, Roger Lansley, used to have a phrase for this: 'Don't confuse me with facts, my mind is made up.'

Most career changers love tests, boxes and checklists because their mind is saying 'I feed the data in here, and the answer pops out *here*'. We all love that idea of a magic button, which is why formal testing is so dangerous in career development. It's so easy to sit back passively and wait for a computer or test to tell us the job we should do next. Most dangerous of all, in my estimation, are computer programs that sample your interests and aspirations and then give you a list of job titles. First of all, this kind of test cannot identify what really motivates and interests you. Secondly, no careers test can keep track of the huge range of jobs that are available in the workplace. Tests should only ever be used as a way of seeking alternative possibilities, and never as a way of narrowing choices.

We feel that our thinking should follow a logical sequence:

This may look a little like scientific investigation, but science is a rather slippery model for thinking. In the twentieth century scientists learned that there are few certainties and an infinite number of strange possibilities. Light appears to behave as both a particle and a wave. Heisenberg's uncertainty principle means that we can no longer say where something is and what it is doing at the same time. Quantum theory blurs notions of common sense and logic, while relativity challenges any secure notions we have about space and time.

Problems cannot be solved at the same level of awareness that created them.

Albert Einstein

On first impression, having too many alternatives seems a recipe for indecision and vagueness. One of the great tools to business creativity is the process of brainstorming, but this is often misused because the process is cut off halfway through. Brainstorming is a good way of generating a large number of ideas in a free-flowing, non-critical environment. The effect is rather like a shotgun blast – both broad and inaccurate. What any brainstorming session needs (and this will apply to your own creative thinking applied to the career process) is a secondary tool to help you to prioritize, test ideas, group ideas together and focus on the next step (see my discussion of De Bono's six thinking hats in Chapter 8).

Switching fields: the practicalities

It's worth bearing in mind a few simple truths about career change:

1. It is relatively straightforward to change occupations and remain within the same field. For example, you may remain in secondary school education but become an administrator rather than a teacher.

2. It is relatively straightforward to switch fields but remain in the same occupation. You may want to remain an accountant, and switch from manufacturing to the hotel trade.

3. The hardest shift is to change both occupation and field at the same time. Don't believe those negative voices that tell you this is impossible. You just need better research, and a better strategy for finding out what's really out there. Sometimes it's worth thinking about a stepping-stone approach: change one element now, and another in, say, 12 months' time, when you have gained some relevant experience.

What work I have done I have done because it has been play. If it had been work I shouldn't have done it.

Mark Twain

> ### Jane's story
>
> Jane had spent 10 years building up a successful computer consultancy. Her quality of life was excellent, her products were cutting edge. However, Jane recognized that there was something missing.
>
> Jane sold her business and now runs two restaurants. When I asked her why she eventually decided to switch from the field of computing solutions to the restaurant trade, she answered, 'I love food, and I love being in restaurants. But the real reason was that I wanted to work in a field where *I can see customers enjoying themselves*. My computer clients were satisfied, but the service I provided hardly ever bought a smile to their faces.'

If you want to achieve a career breakthrough it's vital that you commit some time to exploring your fields of interest. If some of the following exercises make you feel uncomfortable or seem unconventional, then it means they're working. Field exploration is about putting aside the rulebook and discovering new ways of thinking.

EXERCISE 9.1 – MOVING FROM SUBJECTS TO FIELDS

Step 1: Listing the subjects that interest you

1. Begin with the **subjects** you are interested in. Use the House of Knowledge exercise in Chapter 6 to identify all of the subjects you have ever been interested in. Write them all down.

2. Pick your **top 20 subjects**. Do this by asking yourself the question 'Which subjects am I most interested in?' At this

stage don't think about work, just think about the subjects you would like to know more about.

3. Transfer your top subjects on to **20 cards**; use cards about the same size as a playing card, or blank postcards.

4. **Review your cards** by discarding anything that is essentially a repetition of something else. Combine any duplicated or very similar fields. You may have *Product Design* and *Design* – perhaps they would be better as one card.

5. **Add cards** to get a total of 20. Think again: 'What would I like to know more about/study/think about/spend time discussing … ?

Step 2: Refocusing on fields

6. Review your top 20 cards, splitting them into two columns:

Primary fields	**Other fields**
Fields I would like some contact with through work during the next 12 months	Fields which I found interesting, but don't need to be part of my work during the next 12 months

7. Look at the cards you have placed in the Primary fields column, and **choose your top 10**.

8. Look at your top 10 carefully. Redefine any fields that are too **vague**: 'Management' or 'Administration' or 'Company Director' – these are roles that can be exercised in virtually any occupational field.

9. You have now arrived at your **top 10 fields for investigation**.

10. Check: **are your fields too big**? If so, they will not be helpful to you. People tend to select too wide a field, assuming that this will lead to a wider range of opportunities. In fact, what it leads to is a vagueness which quickly communicates itself to recruiters. If necessary, **convert fields into subfields**. For example, if your field is Marketing, ask yourself whether there are any particular fields where you like to exercise marketing. Are you more inter-

ested in marketing products or services? Do your interests lie in advertising, direct mail, brand development or at a strategic level? Are you more interested in marketing one kind of product or service than another?

Step 3: Field combining

11. Look at the **connections** between fields. Move your cards round on a table or notice board to see what happens when you combine them. Try grouping your fields in different ways.

12. Take three of your chosen fields and put them in a row. Then take three more and put them in a column. Draw a 3 × 3 grid of nine squares between the two. In each of your nine blank squares write down any new fields or subfields that come to mind. An example is shown in Figure 9.1.

	Physical fitness	Translating	Export/import
Creative writing	Writing self-help books to encourage fitness	Translating novels	Writing export guides
Safety management	Organizing safety in physical fitness programmes	Specialist translation of safety management material	Exporting best practice in safety
Ecotourism	Environmentally friendly mountain biking	Translating commercial tourism ideas into ecotourism	Importing ecotourism models from other cultures

Figure 9.1 Example 3 × 3 field grid

Step 4: Putting ideas into action

13. Now begins a key step: **research**. Research the key information about these fields (entry routes, qualifications and training you need, measures for success, prospects). Talk to people actually working in these fields to find out what the job is really like.

14. Once you have researched your top five or six fields, come back to this exercise. You will probably find that field exploration leads you to redefine and adapt your working list. Don't think of your fields list as definitive or fixed; think of it as a work in progress.

EXERCISE 9.2 – THE LOTUS BLOSSOM TECHNIQUE

(Based on an idea developed by Yasuo Matsumura.)

In this technique, you place any **field** idea in the centre of a blank Lotus Blossom grid (see Figure 9.2). Then think of eight parallel, related, contrasting or complementary fields – add anything that feels exciting or useful. Write them in the empty boxes around. Each of those new fields then becomes the centre of another 'petal'. This works well on a very big sheet of paper.

Entertainment	Media	Writing
Community advice	Law	Mergers & acquisitions
Resolving conflict	Negotiating	Property

Figure 9.2 One field into eight

Each of your new connections then becomes the centre of another web of ideas, as indicated in Figure 9.3, which shows the original petal centred on 'Law' and a new petal starting with 'Resolving conflict'. Each grey cell can now be opened out to generate eight new possibilities, generating 80 from

		Journalism			Media		Journalism	
					Entertainment		Media	
					Community advice	Law	Mergers & acquisitions	Mergers & acquisitions
					Resolving conflict	Negotiating	Property	
	Entertainment					Negotiating		Property
			Counselling					
	Community advice	Resolving conflict	Personality assessment					
	Violence at work	Risk assessment	Arbitration					
Team building	Marriage guidance	Industrial relations						

Figure 9.3 Lotus Blossom grid

your original single thought. It is, of course, possible to open the petal out even further and create hundreds of connected ideas, but it's also productive to begin again with one key word at the heart of a new 9 × 9 grid.

'MUST DO' LIST

☑ Don't ignore the power of fields when searching for a job you'll love.

☑ Don't allow 'Yes, but' thinking to prevent further investigation of a field that interests you.

☑ Don't miss out the step of looking at the subjects that interest you. Find out what you have really been interested in, often outside work.

☑ Look back at your working life. What fields have you found most satisfying? Why?

☑ Draw up a prioritized list of fields that appeal to you. Set out a plan to investigate more about them.

☑ Write down your top three Job Themes. If you combine those three together, what ideas do you come up with?

☑ Look for field ideas in unexpected places which say something about you: your bookshelves, your photograph albums, articles you have clipped from newspapers.

☑ Become a future watcher. Read articles about how the world of work is changing. See how many new fields and new job titles you can discover.

☑ Don't be put off if you can't find fields which interest you – it just means that you need a new way of looking.

Do You Need a Complete Change of Career?

This chapter helps you to:

▌ Rethink the way you choose your career

▌ Explore field combinations

▌ Map out fields you would like to actively research

▌ Take the first steps towards a total change of career

Your imagination is your preview of life's coming attractions.
Albert Einstein

I want a complete change of career

Firstly, let's deal with the 'change of career' notion. Many careers specialists argue that in fact we only have one career, populated by a range of experiences which include work, learning, personal development, interests and activity outside work. In fact, you operate better at interview if you talk in these terms rather than apologizing for 'changing career' or 'switching paths' or any other loaded language which implies there's only one, conventional way of having a career.

So how do you begin if you want to add more colour, more variety to your single, integrated career path? Here's an interesting fact about the world of careers advice. People prefer to buy careers books with the words 'interview' or 'CV' or 'job search' in the title. However, when it comes to asking for help, most enquirers begin with a statement like 'I would like to find out what else I could do' or 'I have a feeling I want to do something completely different'.

People ask for help in this situation because making a career change is much tougher than making a job change. It's a journey into the unfamiliar that might require new information, new ways of thinking, and will almost certainly require a very strong CV and interview performance. Because a career change increases the degree of risk you will face, it also means increasing the chances of falling flat on your face – confidence and a creative career strategy become more important than ever. So, in fact, many areas already touched on by this book are already helping you if you would like to try a very different career path. You have already looked at your constraints, examined your personality, skill set and knowledge base, and looked at the activities in life and sectors that give you a sense of fulfillment. That's where you begin. This chapter will take you forward so you start looking at – and acting upon – completely new options.

How do we decide on a career path?

When I have a first session with a client I want to know a few basic things – past, present, and future. What has motivated this person in the past, both within work and outside it? What was the best job? The best organization? Then the focus shifts to 'what next?' People usually begin by stating that they have no idea about what they want to do next, but they usually do. I think it was the US careers specialist Dick Knowdell who stated that everyone, in fact, knows exactly what they want to do in life. The problem, he says, is this: one half doesn't know how to describe what they're looking for, while the other half knows what they want but is too frightened to say it.

The most interesting – and demanding – question you will ever have to deal with if you go to see a career coach is not 'what are you going to do next?' or even 'how are you going to get it', but 'how are you going to decide?' Most people secretly believe that the answer will just come along if you take a test, read a book, or just sit at home long enough with the curtains closed and think really, really hard.

Let's backtrack slightly. How do we choose our career paths? As Chapter 9 reveals, we are initially funnelled into fields of work by academic choices. It's worth looking at a range of other strong and typical influences:

Typical prompts to career choice

Parental expectations – occupational groups tend to repeat themselves in families

Parental aspirations – pushing young people towards high pay, high status occupations such as law, medicine or finance

Peer pressure – doing something cool, avoiding things that look boring

Your boss's advice – insider information on scaling the career ladder – the advice of your very first boss is very influential

Personal values and beliefs – the kind of work that seems worthwhile

Media influence – the jobs we see done on TV or in films or on YouTube

Teachers and lecturers – because of the effect of educational 'funnelling'

Careers Advisers – particularly influential while you are also making study choices

---

> **Work-related tests** – ranging from *bona fide* personality or interest inventories to something you found on the Internet
>
> **Personal vocational choice** – your strong or vague sense of what might work, what you are 'supposed' to be doing, or what you feel called to in life.

We understand jobs that touch our lives frequently, for example a GP or dentist. But do you know what a systems analyst does, or a risk assessor, or a behavioural psychologist or a voice coach? In our modern economy, new types of jobs are created every day. Most will be invisible to us, and we have to rely on hunches, insider information or assumptions to choose between them.

Some jobs are more visible than others. You know what a surgeon, a barrister or a fire-fighter does. Or, you think you do – how much of your perception is based on television roles rather than the way people really do their jobs?

The power of the media on career choice cannot be underestimated. Television, in particular, samples the world of work in a very slanted way. Some jobs are shown frequently (doctors, pathologists, teachers, detectives, gardeners and shop assistants), others almost never (prizes offered for anyone who has seen any of the following jobs portrayed within TV fiction: order pickers, people who pack chilled or frozen food, 3-D designers, furniture makers, opticians, car valeters). Interestingly some jobs that never appear are also linked to national shortages, for example chiropodists and civil engineers. Some occupations in the same sector are given very different weighting – TV loves architects but tends to ignore surveyors. Headhunters are often shown, career coaches virtually never.

Editing also happens in another way. When you see a police officer portrayed on TV, either in fiction or in a documentary, what is shown? Normally chasing, apprehending or cautioning a member of the public. If you talk to actual police officers you discover that even those on the 'beat' spend most of their time checking emails or completing paperwork. TV prefers the more exciting moments: the airline pilot avoiding a crash, the nurse dealing with an angry patient, or the ambulance crew saving a patient's life.

In fact, television shapes the way we see jobs more than anything else. We work on the assumption that viewers can tell the difference between television and reality. Worryingly, more than a few can't. The actor Johnny Briggs played the factory owner Mike Baldwin in *Coronation Street* for 30 years. Every week he received a handful of genuine job applications seeking work in his fictional factory. Even more worryingly, about once a week someone applied for the job of assistant manager.

Deciding what or who?

The trouble with most of the careers advice we receive as young people is that most of it revolves around the question 'What do you want to **do** when you grow up?' We are supposed to look thoughtful, and then come up with a job title: 'Er ... a ... Chartered Accountant!'

A more authentic decision might be about what kind of person you hope to be. So, many people, particularly those taking a more spiritual view of life choices, say that the most important thing is about who you are, not what you do. Others will say that it's self-indulgent to focus on the individual, and more practical to focus on the work that is actually available.

The answer, I believe, is like so many of the most important truths in life, a matter of holding conflicting ideas in your mind at the same time, as the career spectrum model in Figure 10.1 makes clear.

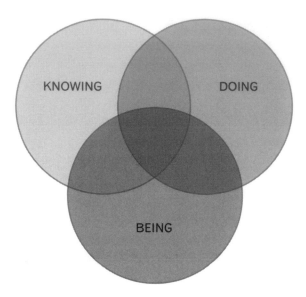

Figure 10.1   Career spectrum

The first step to a complete career change takes very little time at all. Draw a larger version of the above three circles for yourself, and within each circle write in the key words that capture what's important for you, right now, using the paragraphs below if you need a nudge.

Knowing

In Chapter 6 we revealed the way that *what you choose to know about* provides powerful clues about the kind of work that will seem meaningful. So if you are considering a complete change of career, it's worth thinking carefully about the kind of topics you would like to read or talk about while you are at work. Secondly, review all the things you know about so you have a clear idea of the underpinning knowledge you may need to demonstrate for handling competency-based interviews (see Chapter 12).

Understanding the knowledge angle of work is also an insight into your motivation, both now and in the future, because it treats each job as a learning curve. Most roles are interesting in their first few weeks or months, but whether a job is intrinsically interesting in the long run is often about how much you will continue to learn and grow.

We are what we repeatedly do.

Aristotle

Doing

Aristotle's words above might be rephrased *what we choose to do matters*. The activities that take up most of our waking hours have a strong influence on our effectiveness, the outcomes our work generates, and the way people see us. Remember that word 'occupation'? A job is what 'occupies' our time and attention. Skills are powerful reinforcers of self-esteem and are the best way of making our values tangible in the world by getting things done. Skills need refreshing and updating, but more than anything else they need to be used. Using only part of your skill set, or using skills you really don't value very much, can lead to long-term demotivation and cynicism.

Refer to Chapter 7 to refresh and build on your understanding of what you do regularly and well in terms of behaviours, skills and competences.

Being (and valuing)

How you exercise the skills you have is very dependent on your attitude and values, two factors which are strongly linked to personality. To perform a task well, accurately, with care, taking into account the needs of other people, to be able to meet deadlines, to be cheerful or resourceful under pressure, these are all aspects of personality that you should revisit through the various opportunities offered in this book, notably in Chapter 8.

The question of 'being' is not just about the personality you were born with, but also a big clue about values. During life we also build up a sense of what is important to us. Some of those things are clearly demonstrated through the things we choose to learn about under the 'know' heading, but others are deeper still. Think about the causes or charities you support (whether with time, money or sympathy). What issues energize you? What makes you angry?

Exploring your values in more detail

Try the **Values Comparator** in Table 10.1. List the different kinds of work you have considered up to now (including the jobs you never got round to applying for). What values are expressed through the outcomes achieved through those jobs (e.g. helping others, delivering a quality service, providing value for money, providing a good experience, etc.). So, for example, you might say of a sales job that the main outcome was 'increasing sales turnover' and the value expressed was 'putting profit ahead of quality' and, having given that a zero score, you will record 'providing high quality products at the right price'. Alternatively the main outcome of another job might be 'becoming market leader', with the implied value being 'setting the standard' and your score of 3 confirming your own personal value 'working for a reputable organization capable of making an impact'.

Table 10.1 – Values Comparator

My past and present jobs What **outcomes** and **implied values** were expressed in this job?	**My score for each implied value, scale 0–3**	Scoring Your Implied Values 0 These outcomes seem of no value to me 1 These outcomes are a weak match to my personal values 2 These outcomes seem of value, but I can't get too excited about them 3 These outcomes match my personal values
Job 1 Outcome:	Score:	My personal value statement:
Implied value:		
Job 2 Outcome:	Score:	My personal value statement:
Implied value:		
Job 3 Outcome:	Score:	My personal value statement:
Implied value:		

CAREER CHANGE: STARTING FROM THE INSIDE OUT

What calls you?

Are you looking for a role which is more of a vocation than a job? The word 'vocation' comes from the Latin *vocare*, 'to call'. In popular usage a 'vocation' feels different to an occupation. A vocation is something we feel 'called' to do – in other words, a sense of commitment that is stronger than ordinary levels of motivation. A vocation is seen as a job, either professional or voluntary, that is carried out more for its altruistic benefit than for income. The term can also be used to describe any occupation for which a person is specifically gifted, and usually implies that the individual's sense of calling towards the task in hand has been recognized by others.

There is an additional and often forgotten dimension: it should be a good experience. 'Good experience' isn't the same as 'fun', but shouldn't be a million miles from it. Peter Sinclair, leader of the 'After Sunday' movement, is fond of reminding people that one of the indicators of vocation is enjoyment – receiving and expressing joy as a result of activity. If the job makes you miserable, can it really be a vocation? Having said that, there are an awful lot of glum-looking people holding down clergy, teaching, nursing or charity roles we would normally describe as more of a vocation than a job. This isn't to say that every job should be enjoyable all the time, but work should perhaps enrich the person conducting it at least half of the working week. And, secondly, the sense of 'calling' isn't just about being individualistic. After all, many vocations arise out of a strong sense of personal values (see earlier in this chapter) or a sense of service. Finally, just to put the word back into the context of faith from which it reaches us, the most important thing about 'calling' is not the individual being called, but the calling itself. Whether driven by a sense of human need or greater purpose, responding to our call may be a duty, not an indulgence.

CAREER CHANGE: STARTING FROM THE OUTSIDE IN

Look again at the field choices prompted by Chapter 9, particularly from the Job Themes discussion (Table 9.1).

Are you sure you don't know what you want to do? Begin, as suggested above, with the question *If all jobs paid the same, what would you do?* Then try on the question *Which jobs would you like to try out just for a week?*

Look again at what's out there, using Chapter 9 to assist you to map fields of work. Try the following expanding sequence:

1. Fields of work you know well

2. Sectors and sub-sectors that have intersected with your job

3. Fields you have had some contact with during your career

4. Fields you know something about through your personal interests, friends or commitments.

At this stage, try not to allow 'Yes, but' thinking to get in the way. You don't have to make a decision at this stage – all you are doing is generating ideas. Here some other tried and tested prompts to get you to generate job ideas:

▎ Think of people you know who are doing interesting jobs. What's interesting about them?

▎ What jobs have you applied for in the past but didn't get?

▎ What jobs have you seen advertised that caught your attention for 30 seconds, even if you did nothing about them?

Go back to your House of Knowledge (see Chapter 6). The clues are all there in the topics that have called you, year after year. Somewhere in a box, in your loft or under the stairs, there's a box with the evidence: those projects that keep coming out every 2–3 years. Look, too, at the things you have chosen to study over the years.

Refer back to Exercise 9.1 to look at the way you can move from subjects that interest you generally in life to fields of work. Use the exercise to brainstorm field ideas.

Don't get hung up on another job myth: that if you try to turn a hobby into a living you will fall out of love with it. Plenty of people are busy being paid to do things which they would happily do for nothing in their own time. Starting with subjects means starting with enthusiasm and energy. Remember the origin of the word enthusiast – 'filled with God'. The apparently trivial things that fill us with happiness are often big clues about the kinds of activities which feed the soul.

You might also want to try out a few more exercises which force you to use lateral thinking to answer the question 'whatever next?' Exercises 10.1 and 10.2 are designed to do exactly that.

CAREER CHANGE: JUST PLAIN STARTING

As this chapter has rehearsed, the question is not how you are going to find a new career, but how you are going to decide. Thinking things through matters. Re-imagining the possibilities of your career makes all the difference.

The next big question is *what are you going to do about it?* The second half of this book provides several prompts to activity, but let's nail down one plain fact. If you want to put off career change forever (or at least until it's too late) then keep on reflecting, analysing and mulling over. Keep on thinking that you have to make the perfect decision before you act. That will happily put change off forever.

However, if you don't want to be spending your last inactive years saying 'I wish', then do something. Finding out, following your enthusiasm, costs very little. You don't need to have a perfect target job to start the process of discovery – just a sense of curiosity. And here's a big clue: your breakthrough has a 5%

likelihood of happening as a result of reading or thinking, and a 95% likelihood of arriving as a result of a person. Someone you already know, possibly. Or, even more likely, someone you meet in the next 2–3 months as a result of your active enquiries. So don't neglect to use the tried and tested REVEAL method of informational interviews (see Appendix 1) and, for a quick start, act upon the Career Change Action Checklist given at the end of this chapter for immediate action.

THE FIELD GENERATOR

EXERCISE 10.1 – USING THE FIELD GENERATOR TO MOVE FROM INTERESTS TO FIELDS

As Chapter 1 indicates, sometimes it is necessary to use provocative thinking to generate ideas and make new connections. The Field Generator in Figure 10.2 begins with what you know and your primary areas of interest, and then moves you through a thinking process that should help you to generate unexpected ideas about potential fields of work.

If you are short of field ideas, go back to the House of Knowledge exercise in Chapter 6. Use a highlighter pen to mark your preferred interests. Now refer to the Field Generator in Figure 10.2.

The brain is a wonderful organ. It starts working the moment you get up in the morning and does not stop until you get to work

Robert Frost

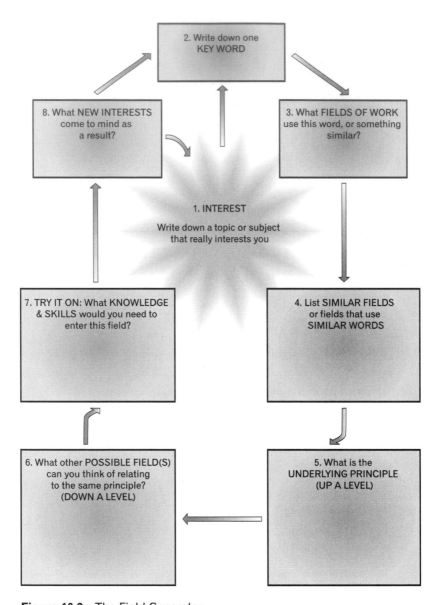

Figure 10.2   The Field Generator

	How to use the Field Generator
Step 1	Take copies of Figure 10.2, the Field Generator, and try this exercise out using as many interests as you can. This exercise works best with someone else working with you, prompting and asking questions. Make sure you have completed the House of Knowledge exercise in Chapter 6. Pick five or six of your strongest interests. Write one of your interests in **Box 1**, e.g. boats, sailing and the sea.
Step 2	In **Box 2** write down a key word from your area of interest, e.g. sailing.
Step 3	Look at your key word and in **Box 3** write down three fields of work where this word appears, e.g. sailing instruction, sailing boat design, sailing restoration.
Step 4	Now that you have expanded your field a little, think of fields of work that use similar words, and write them in **Box 4**, e.g. ship building, naval architecture, merchant navy, navigation. Make a note in the margin of any new fields that you hadn't thought of before that are maybe connected in some way with your interest, e.g. outward-bound training, water safety.
Step 5	This is where you have a chance to use a technique which in idea-building terms is called 'going up a level'. Look at your fields in Box 4. Is there any overriding category that describes them? If you were to find these ideas together in one drawer, what label would you put on the front of the drawer? (e.g. nursing and osteopathy can be placed within the general category of 'medicine' or 'physiology'). This may take a while to work out, or you may think of several alternatives. The answer will be unique to you. In this case you might come up with weather, racing, healthy competition, low technology, getting away from it all, being captain of my own boat .... What is the underlying 'big idea'? Write down your final answer in **Box 5**, e.g. healthy competition might be your preferred underlying principle here.
Step 6	In Box 5 we moved up a level to the underlying principle. In **Box 6** we come down a level at a different point. In this case you might come up with something totally unconnected to sailing arising from 'healthy competition', e.g. sports coaching, teaching kids about diet and exercise, or teaching fund-raising skills to charity staff, or selling ethical financial products. Write down any ideas that appeal to you, making sure you don't try to exclude them at this stage by misguided thinking about what is 'practical'. You may discover fields or new interests here that could one day become part of your House of Knowledge.
Step 7	Underline one of the fields or ideas generated in Box 6, and write it in **Box 7**. It's probably best to begin with one that has surprised you most (e.g. in this case you might have come up with teaching fund-raising skills to charity staff). Write down what you feel to be the key skills and knowledge that you would need to work in this field. Begin by putting down what you already know, and add more by putting yourself mentally into the shoes of someone working in this area. The only way to build up an accurate picture is to find out. Ask someone already working in this field, or do some desk research. If this step was productive and interesting, go back to Box 6 and do the same again with any other interesting fields.
Step 8	**Box 8** allows you to record any new areas of interest that the exercise might have brought up, e.g. coaching. Take a new copy of the Field Generator and put this new interest in Box 1, and begin again. A completed Field Generator is shown in Figure 10.3.

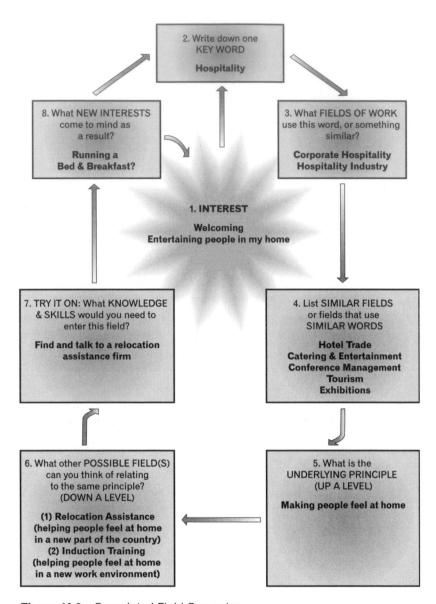

Figure 10.3 Completed Field Generator

EXERCISE 10.2 – DISCONTINUOUS THINKING

This process is great for times when you are completely stuck for ideas, and works well alongside the Field Generator. Discontinuous thinking is about provoking your mind into making new connective pathways. It's the driving force behind Edward de Bono's concept of provocative thinking, and also one of the characteristics of Roger Van Oech's delightfully off-the-wall book *A Whack on the Side of the Head*.

There are few rules with this kind of exercise. One of the principles behind it is that you think about something else entirely, and then allow some kind of connection or comparison between your thought process and your main problem. Here are some ideas that might work particularly well with fields:

1. *Try a provocative statement which sounds deliberately illogical or nonsensical.* For example 'a field which is about persuading and influencing but avoids people'. This might take you into ways of translating your interpersonal skills into text-based or alternative contexts, e.g. writing to influence, finding great words for websites, writing other people's speeches, designing models for negotiation and conflict management that can be communicated by distance learning. Another one might be 'building houses that nobody will live in' – you might apply your construction skills to buildings used for housing animals or equipment; you might start building models rather than sketching things out in words; you might create 'virtual' libraries, supermarkets or conference centres on the Internet.

2. *Try turning your field upside down.* For example, you may be interested in child development because you are interested in the way young people grow. Turning that upside down might lead you to thinking about the way older people degenerate. This may be a field which interests you in itself, or it may help you to refocus on your chosen field, e.g. by looking at the effects of head injury in young people.

'MUST DO' LIST

Your checklist for beginning a career change TODAY

KNOWING	1) Review your House of Knowledge (Chapter 6).
	2) Review your preferred Job Themes (see Table 9.1)
	3) Look seriously at the things *that you have chosen to know about*, and your favourite subjects.
	4) Use the exercises in this book, including the Field Generator, to translate these ideas into potential fields of work.
DOING	5) Review your skills using either the first impression list in Table 7.1 or any of the more detailed skill exercises in Chapter 7.
	6) Consider using the JLA Skill Cards to identify your motivated skills.
BEING	7) Look at the values and preferences expressed in your Jigsaw Job (Exercise 5.1)
	8) List your top three Career Hot Buttons (see Chapter 5)
	9) Draw out any relevant personality-related material from Chapter 8.
	10) Complete the **Values Comparator** (Table 10.1)
NEXT STEPS	11) Put together the above information on one sheet of A4 (the master sheet in Figure 16.1 provides a useful template). Now STOP reflecting and move into action steps, namely:
	12) Show your results to friends and colleagues. Ask for ideas and connections.

13) Give people an idea of what you are looking for – use the One Sentence Message in Chapter 16.

14) Write down five potential target fields. They don't need to be perfect. Use the REVEAL method from the end of this book to generate meetings with interesting people.

Creative Job Search Strategies

This chapter helps you to:

❙ Debunk job-hunting myths

❙ Discover the hidden job market

❙ Anticipate employer risk aversion

❙ Research before you search

❙ Build your personal web

An idea is nothing more nor less than a new combination of old evidence.

James Webb Young

MYTH-CRACKING

One of my strangest discoveries when I moved from training recruiters to assisting career builders was that there really are some fairly well-kept secrets about the way people get jobs. It's also true that people restrict their job-hunting strategy within limits defined by **job-hunting myths**.

If you've been waiting for the moment when you felt you got your money's worth, this may be it. Job-hunting myths are explored and debunked in Table 11.1.

Table 11.1 Job hunting: myth or fact?

What your mother/careers teacher/best friends told you	Job market reality
Jobs are filled by people applying for published vacancies.	About 20–30% of jobs are filled in this way (less in executive markets).
It's easier to get a job when you have one already.	True to a point: employers like to bet on certainties, not outsiders, so they want a recent track record. If you have 'problems' with your CV, you need to have a good narrative ready to cover gaps, changes of direction, 'unemployment' (is it really unemployment if you are learning or extending your skills?).
It's who you know, not what you know.	Making connections will increase your chance of being seen. Employers buy experience and potential, so at interview they will be far more impressed with what you can do than who you know, unless it's the kind of job where you're supposed to bring contacts and clients with you.
Qualifications count.	Employers often have a blinkered view of what qualifications they need. The key question is: what is the standard for the job or industry? If yours are a little light, don't over-highlight them on your CV, and stress the intellectual standards you have achieved through your work experience. If you have constantly turned your back on opportunities to extend your knowledge and training, you need to have a pretty good reason.

You need good references.	Very few employers use reference checking to screen applicants before interview. Mostly references are a final check and need not be included on your CV unless requested.
Send as many CVs out as you can.	Do you know how many employment agencies push out CVs every day? How much time do you think a busy manager will give to a speculative CV where there is no obvious connection to the company's needs? Five seconds? Speculative letters and CVs *do* work (far better with employers than with recruitment consultants) and give you access to the hidden job market, but only if they are extremely well targeted and followed up by personal contact.
Sometimes you have to push yourself forward.	'Sometimes'? It's the idea of 'pushing' that puts people off, as if you are advertising something shoddy. Don't claim to be what you are not, but in everything you do, present the best version of yourself, and a clear message of what you can do for others. Try it as a way of life, not just job search.
Only pushy people get jobs through networking.	Not true. Networking works for everyone as long as they do it positively and honestly. See below for more on networking.
A job's a job. Think of the money. Good jobs are hard to find.	OK, red card. Go back to Chapter 1. Do not pass Go. Do not collect £200.

THE HIDDEN JOB MARKET

Insanity is doing the same thing over and over and expecting a different result.

Eva May Brown

The majority of jobs are not advertised. If you only ever respond to job advertisements, you'll never know about them. This is the hidden job market. Many job hunters are unaware of it; most don't know how to break into it.

You can look at the hidden job market in two ways: right or left brain.

First of all, food for the imagination. If you want to slow down your job search and limit your options (maybe somebody is paying you to fail?) then act on the negative myths in Table 11.1 and limit your job search to advertised positions. You'll miss out on most newly created jobs, all positions filled by word of mouth, and most jobs with small, energetic compa nies. You'll miss out on all those companies that are just on the edge of thinking about creating a new job. You'll never have a chance to be recommended by a friend or colleague.

Secondly, for all you people who need to see the numbers, Table 11.2 records the way that people in the UK find jobs. These data are based on a UK survey of workers who had been with their employer for 3 months or less at the time of interview.

Table 11.2 How people find jobs

Method	Men	Women
Reply to an advertisement	24.2%	31.6%
Hearing from someone who worked there	31.3%	25.3%
Direct application	14.1%	15.6%
Private employment agency or business	10.3%	9.4%
Job centre	9.0%	7.3%
Some other way	10.7%	10.3%

Figures relating to the UK Labour market in 2002 from
http://www.statistics.gov.uk/StatBase

Using job boards and the Internet

Don't exclude any job search method, because the most effective overall strategy is to use every tool in your toolbox. The Internet can be a great source of information, but statistically it is the least effective method. However there are some excellent job boards out there, many of them packed with information and advice. You will also find it useful to look at employer job boards – where you may come across jobs you don't see advertised elsewhere. In general, job boards work best for workers whose skills can be communicated quickly in key words (e.g. computer programmers). They are best used as part of a multi-strategy approach: use job boards to work out salary levels, to spot employers and to identify recruitment consultants you can telephone. Appendix 3 contains a list of websites useful for online job hunting and career development.

A word of warning: many job-seekers love using the Internet. It takes little effort, it's relatively passive, yet it looks like activity. Job seekers in the USA are often given a clear instruction by career coaches: don't use the Internet during working hours. The problem with spending all day staring at a screen is that it's a great excuse for not doing the most important thing: talking to people. The Internet makes a great tool for researching organizations, but it's a poor job search method. An email is forgotten within about 15 minutes, but a telephone call sticks in the memory for several days, while a good face-to-face discussion can be remembered for months if you follow it up effectively.

EMPLOYER SAFETY HABITS

Here's another tip that in itself probably justifies the cover price of this book: employers and job seekers use totally opposite strategies to achieve the same result – filling a job. Table 11.3 illustrates how employers prefer to recruit, and why.

Table 11.3 Employer risk aversion

Employer's preference	Risk level to the employer	Employer thinking
Almost family Somebody we already know: an internal appointment is ideal, or someone already doing consultancy or temp work for us.	Virtually risk free	We know exactly what we're getting.
Known quantity Maybe someone working for a competitor, someone whose reputation we know even if we haven't met the individual yet.	Very low	A clear track record. This person has done well elsewhere and will do the same for us.
A friend of a friend In other words, someone who is known and trusted by someone we know and trust, or someone who comes highly recommended by a trusted colleague.	Low	We have a pretty good idea of what we will be getting. Fred always recommends good people.
Achiever Someone who may be known to us at a distance, and comes with clear evidence of past success – ideally in terms of a portfolio of work, a fistful of testimonials, excellent and highly specific projects with their names all over them.	Relatively low	Again, clear evidence of past achievement. We can measure what we'll be getting for our money.

Employer's preference	Risk level to the employer	Employer thinking
Competence-based recruitment We've accurately assessed what a successful post holder must know and the skills required by the job, and we are going to test or interview to identify specific competences.	Controlled	We're using a careful filter, trying to predict workplace performance. We would still like to know what candidates are like in terms of personality and team fit.
Unsolicited application This is much more than yet another CV sent out on a 'spray and pray' basis. A well-aimed direct application can sometimes prompt an employer to do something about a new job, or solve an old problem.	Moderately high (but potentially low risk if it's the right person)	We are now talking to strangers, but sometimes it's nice to be surprised by the right people. We're more impressed by people who know something about us already, particularly if we have a problem right now. In fact, if we get to talk to this person and like what we see, we'll reclassify them as 'achievers' or even 'friends'.
Attractive agency candidate OK, we'll talk to an employment agency or recruitment consultant at this point, because they know where to resource people who have done well in the past, and they can screen for us. They can	Risk increasing	Agencies don't always know as much as they should do about the actual requirements of the job, and they sometimes pigeon-hole candidates. However, they are very good at giving feedback about how an employer is likely to react to a CV.

Employer's preference	Risk level to the employer	Employer thinking
sometimes head-hunt people directly.		
Response to specific advertising Who knows if we'll get the right people? *And* we run the risk of buying advertising space without being sure of a result.	High	It's going to be tough to filter out the ones who know what they're doing. Who do we interview? It feels like a lottery.
Response to general recruitment advertising Oh dear. Here we go – hundreds of hopefuls to be filtered out.	Sky high	Nobody reads the skill or qualification requirements, nobody filters these people, and they're all desperate to get a job.

Table 11.4 shows the mirrored position for the job seeker, outlining job seeker assumptions and comparing them with the market reality.

MAKING GOOD USE OF RECRUITMENT CONSULTANTS

It's vital to remember that although most recruitment consultants keep a bank of potentially suitable applicants, they are largely vacancy driven. That means that they are most interested in you if you are a quick fit for a vacancy that needs filling immediately. However, consultancies do have an extremely good feel for the market, and where they deal with specialist fields, the information they can give you can be priceless.

Table 11.4   Job seeker thinking

Activity	Job seeker's thinking	Market reality
Response to advertising Hours spent filling in application forms, drafting a letter of application, sprucing up the CV. A quiet prayer or a philosophical shrug as the envelope goes in the post, then the waiting begins. It's useful to remember that someone will be short listing, probably into three piles: *No*, *Possible* and *Yes*. Have you done everything you can do to get on to the *Yes* pile?	**My big chance** Great, a chance to show off my CV, list my skills. The more information I can give, the more they'll be impressed. Now all I have to do is put a stamp on the envelope and cross my fingers.	**Small chance** How many other applications hit the desk in the same post? How differentiated is your message? How do you convince the employer that you are worth talking to in person – particularly in comparison with internal or recommended candidates? You might improve the odds if you follow up your application with a telephone call. Many advisers say you should *always* ring to confirm that your application has been seen.

Unsolicited application
This is much more than yet another CV sent out on a 'spray and pray' basis. A well-aimed direct application can sometimes prompt an employer to do something about a new job, or solve an old problem.

Keep shooting ...
and I'll hit something eventually. At least it gets me noticed.

Long shot ...
if you're firing with a shotgun, but effective if you use a sniper rifle – is the recipient going to be intrigued, pushed to action or irritated at yet another piece of junk mail? It depends on how well targeted your CV is, what the accompanying message has to say, and whether you press the right buttons by knowing something about the needs of the company.

This method is more effectively used in conjunction with personal contact. If someone already knows why you are interesting, your CV gets read.

If this method works you may end up in a shortlist of one – pretty good odds.

Table 11.4 *Contd.*

Activity	Job seeker's thinking	Market reality
Recruitment consultant or employment agency Do your homework – find out which consultants are regularly placing staff in your sector.	**Guiding hands** At last, my chances are in the hands of a recruitment professional, somebody who will help me to develop my career and find me a job. They have all the unadvertised vacancies, don't they?	**Check your assumptions** Agencies make money by placing obvious skills into obvious jobs, not by being career coaches. They receive far more speculative approaches than they can handle. However, an agency interview *can* help you to get a feel for your market worth and check your message to potential employers. Good agencies set up interviews using strong personal contact and recommend you. Poor agencies simply distribute unsolicited CVs. Good agencies will give you focused feedback on your potential. Poor agencies will over-promise and under-deliver. See Chapter 12 for further tips on talking to recruitment consultants.

Achiever	My chance to shine	Collect evidence
In your job, what would be the equivalent of a 'portfolio of work'? How can you present tangible evidence of what you have achieved: brochures, articles, testimonials, records of projects, etc.?	This will really impress them. And it might – as long as what you have to offer matches what the employer needs. The achievement you demonstrate should be a close match to the employer's shopping list, otherwise your prized portfolio is irrelevant.	It's all too easy to make claims about yourself, but you need to back them up with measurable facts. Your CV, and what you say to support your application, and your words at interview, are all *assertions* which you need to support by *evidence*. Keep good records of what you have done: copies of documents, client feedback, affidavits, good appraisals. The more objective the evidence, the lower the perceived risk for the employer.
Competence-based recruitment	**A chance to demonstrate what I can do ...**	**Focus ...**
If you are interviewed, be very clear what you have achieved and how you did it. Even if there is no formal testing, use evidence of achievement to demonstrate the same arguments.	but daunting for many job seekers who are unfamiliar with competence-based interviewing.	on what you know, your skills and your achievements. Be prepared to come up with a range of achievement stories (use the skill clips technique in Chapter 7). Listen for the language that the selector is using so you know which competences are being sought.

Table 11.4 *Contd.*

Activity	Job seeker's thinking	Market reality
Known quantity I get interviewed because of the work I have done in the industry.	**A way in** Keep your eyes and ears open for these opportunities, and make sure people are aware of the contribution you have made as a 'fringe' member of an organization.	**How do you get to be a known quantity?** Simple. Shine. Get to be good at your job and let others know it. Keep a record of your achievements. Write articles or circulate good ideas. Talk with energy to customers, suppliers and sister organizations.
A friend of a friend What I need is someone who can put me on the inside track.	**Who, me? I don't have friends like that** I don't know anybody connected/at the right level/in this field/of that age group, etc. Besides, I'd feel awkward approaching them, and they wouldn't really be able to help me. (See this chapter's section on building a personal web).	**Look around you** Yes, you. Who do you know (not necessarily in work) who admires what you do, and would be happy to recommend you to others? Have you enlisted help from these people as career coaches, dummy interviewers, idea factories? Look around you at family, friends, associates, and find out which ones have pushed opportunities towards others like this. Life has its natural match-makers and fixers, and they love to be known for their contacts and good judgement.

Almost family

I'm happy approaching this kind of company. They feel comfortable talking to me because they already know what I am like.

Old school tie?

This old boy network stuff is unfair or the internal candidate's got a head start. Anyway, how can I possibly get myself known that well to every company I apply to?

Beware of the problems that can arise from informal conversations: the company may not be clear that you are looking for a post, or the conversations may continue endlessly without a clear decision.

Becoming close means becoming wanted

This is *not* about old boy networks – those often produce dreadful appointments. Your research into the *right* fields and companies will get you known as an enthusiast. Work experience, consultancy or simply keeping in touch by sending in good ideas are all strategies that can move you into the target's bull's eye.

If you're not comfortable getting close to these people, you probably don't want to work with them anyway. See below for advice on 'Networking for softies', and also see the REVEAL method in Appendix 1.

Furthermore, a good recruitment consultant will have got to his or her position by knowing a lot of decision makers. A good strategy is to identify about 15–20 recruitment consultants dealing with the kinds of jobs you are after. Find the name of the individual consultant handling this kind of job, and send in a speculative letter with a brief CV. Follow up within 2 days or so with a telephone call, and ask for the opportunity to meet the consultant. Recruitment consultants like to be valued for their industry knowledge, and will often respond well to you if they feel they can learn something from you about organizations or sectors you've worked in.

Many consultants ask you to email in your CV. Remember that an email is remembered for only a few minutes, and your CV attachment may not be opened. Send a posted version in as well.

You will also be asked to register, either online or by filling in an application form. That's fine, but remember that most recruitment consultants admit that they only refer to their database of candidates if they are bored or desperate. Remember that most recruitment consultants are strongly people-oriented. They like to influence, persuade, encourage, and sell. So the key to making the most of a recruitment consultant is for you to establish a good working relationship. You will only do this by having at least one good conversation, ideally face-to-face. If your consultant really understands what you're looking for, remembers you, and believes you will be enthusiastic at interview, you'll get short-listed.

If you get a chance to have an informal interview with a recruitment consultant, try to get a feel for your market worth. Many recruitment consultants have strong views about CV construction, so the best question to ask isn't 'what do you think of my CV?' but 'what does my CV say to you?' A good consultant will also tell you what you are worth in the market-place, and what hurdles you will have to jump if you want to change sector.

BEGINNING A CREATIVE JOB SEARCH

A creative, multi-strategy job search has the following key characteristics:

1. The method draws on all of the following methods:

    *   applications for recognized vacancies

    *   speculative approaches to companies in your chosen fields

    *   personal and professional networking, informational interviews

    *   intelligent use of recruitment consultants

    *   project-based or consultancy work

    *   encouraging an employer to create a new job where one does not already exist.

2. It combines methods effectively to increase their power.

3. You will consciously target the **hidden job market**.

4. You will anticipate **employer risk thinking**.

5. You will be choosing a different strategy to the majority of job seekers.

6. This self-marketing strategy: you are clear what you're selling, and who you're selling to. In other words, you will know who you are, what you are good at and where you want to be. You'll communicate this in a way that broadcasts confidence and a clear message of what you can do for your next employer.

Not networking

I continue to be amazed that career changers, whether recent graduates or experienced executives, hate one activity: networking. Let's check some of their assumptions: 'It's pushy.' 'It's not me.' 'It exploits people and loses you friends.' 'It makes me look desperate.' We should all respect those fears and doubts. Anyone who suggests networking without addressing those issues is selling you a suit that doesn't fit, isn't your colour, and you'll never wear after you take it home.

Networking is something we all do unconsciously. If you move to a new town and want to find a good dentist or know the best local greengrocer, you ask people, casually. If you have problems with your child at school, you ask other parents for recommendations. Networking has been done a huge disservice by people and organizations that exploit the way human networks operate for their own advantage. You know who they are: all those people who want to sell you things you don't really want. The worst kinds use family or professional connections to make you feel guilty enough to buy something.

Personal webs are connections of people. Remember: this doesn't mean trashing any possibility of friendship for the sake of a quick sale or a job offer. It means displaying a genuine interest in others, and an enthusiasm for sharing information. Every person you meet, in your personal life or work life, is part of your personal web. Make connections, but get used to making them as productive as you can – find out what people are looking for, and see whether you can be an information broker. Don't be afraid to ask for the names of others who might be able to help, and always be willing to be an information broker when someone asks *you*.

How the numbers work

People misunderstand the new economy and the idea of networks because they think it's purely about numbers. It isn't. It's about connections. If 4 people are acquaintances, there are 12 one-to-one relationships among them. If you simply add one more person to the group, you get 20 relationships. Six people means 30 connections, and 7 makes 42. As the personal web goes beyond 10, the number of possible interactions explodes.

We're talking about the difference between mailing lists and interest groups. A mailing list may be 1000 separate, unconnected people. An interest group 1000 strong can overturn national policy. Just look at the way a handful of farmers and truck drivers brought the UK to a standstill in the autumn of 2000.

Networking for softies

How can we tap the power of the network economy to assist our career development and job search? Firstly, it's vital to recognize that networking is **not** about getting a job. It's about expanding your range. It's about creating new possibilities. It's about learning more about other jobs, other fields. It's about identifying key people and decision makers.

'Hard-sell' networking never misses a chance to convert a contact to a sale. That's an unsophisticated approach that doesn't fly in the new economy. That approach to using people is as different to building a personal web as cold-call telephone sales differs from being part of an investment club. In a genuine personal web, people are interested in the relationships and in new information, new ideas. They are interested in what new members bring.

Most important of all, **it's not just about you**. The process was once described as a 'chain of helpfulness'. It begins not with the question 'who do I know that I can exploit?', but with 'who do I know that can tell me something interesting?' It may even begin 'who do I know that I can help?' The best personal webs are friendship groups; they are a pool of knowledge rather like the Internet. Everyone puts something in, everyone has a chance to take different things out. Everyone has different needs at different times in their lives. It's often most useful to begin: 'what do I know that would be helpful to others?' It can be something quite ordinary or modest, such as useful web pages, book recommendations, telling people about cheap travel deals or free resources. A chain of helpfulness begins with what you are prepared to give, not what you want to take.

Degrees of separation

You may have come across the theory of **six degrees of separation** (coined, or at least popularized, by the American playwright John Guare). The idea is that anyone can reach anyone else in the world in six jumps. Person A leads you to B, and eventually to your 'target'. You begin by talking to someone who is connected, no matter how tangentially, with the person you're after. Often it's quicker than that. I once saw this explained to a room of MBA students. When the speaker asked for a random example, someone called out 'Nelson Mandela!'. 'What would be the first step if you wanted to speak to Mr Mandela?' A hand shot up near the back: 'Er ... my uncle knows him.' You never know who people know. Unless you ask.

Networking books will tell you about 'working the room' and giving your business card to as many people as you can. That's another huge misunderstanding. Anyone who thinks that networking is about exploiting people has misunderstood the idea of relationships and friendship.

Try finding out what you have in common with the people you talk to, and ask what you can add: what contacts, information, ideas do you have? If others can help you, ask for their assistance honestly. Once you get someone to talk to you, *never* leave them feeling that they haven't helped.

Three predictions

Here are three calculated predictions. The first is the fact that you already know at least one person who can help, really help. When we begin networking for softies we tend to start by scanning the far horizon – people some way off who you know only vaguely. These people will be great contacts, and soon, but first of all you need to take some baby steps. Who do you know who is close by? There's a simple test – you're looking for the kind of person you could pick up the phone and talk to without having to plan what you're going to say.

Play the game backwards. Imagine it is 6 months down the line and you have found your unusual and absorbing job, and think about how you got it. The second prediction is that you will find the job through someone you meet in the next 6 months – a result through a word-of-mouth connection is more likely than by using any other job search method.

The third prediction draws on some exciting work Swiss careers expert Daniel Porot undertook some years back, revealing that the best results come from the third level of networking. The first level is the people you know well. The second level is the people you know vaguely and the people you get introduced to. The third level is largely people you don't know at all right now. Why does the third level work? Possibly because it starts to map out the hidden job market, possibly because the people you meet have no assumptions about you, and possibly because by the time you get to the rich territory of the third level you've got pretty good at the process.

Informational interviews

There are many versions of this idea in print; I believe the original appeared in *What Color is Your Parachute?* The idea is also systematized by Daniel Porot (see *The PIE Method for Career Success*). The principle is straightforward: find someone who knows about a field or occupation in detail, and ask to see them for a short interview during which you ask a series of key questions about entry to the field, rewards and pitfalls, and – most importantly – the names of other people who can give you further assistance.

The important thing to realize is that the technique is about *research, not job search.*

This activity is critically important if you want to access the hidden job market. It helps you to find out the roles and fields which are a great match for your skills and experience, and then helps you to identify target organizations. You may also find that you fall over jobs before they become vacancies. This strategy is so important that it is outlined in detail in Appendix 1: Informational Interviews – The REVEAL Method.

Managing your personal web

It's possible to build up a personal web of between 60 and 100 useful, curious and interesting people within about 3 months. Some principles that will help:

1. Learn how to conduct informational interviews.

2. Start the easy way. Begin with people you know, asking them the question 'Who do you know who works in ...'.

3. Get people to introduce you to other people (see Appendix 1).

4. Build slowly and methodically. Put time aside each week.

5. Keep good records. Use an electronic diary and address book to keep the details. Record the 'hooks', i.e. factors that you have in common. Record the name of your contact's partner or children. Most important of all, use a system that remembers the connections for you. Beyond 40 or so connections your memory will fail. When you're thinking 'who was that designer Bill mentioned?', a programme such as Microsoft Outlook allows you to record links: look up 'Bill Smith' and you will see the names of all Bill's connections.

6. Ask yourself all the time: What can I add to this network? How can I be helpful? Be remembered as a source of information, a person who brings others together.

EXERCISE 11.1 – BEGIN YOUR PERSONAL WEB

First of all, decide what record-keeping system you are going to use so that you can build up a personal web methodically. You'll need full contact information, and be able to cross-link records and keep a note of the areas you discuss. Finally, you'll need a diary reminder of any action or follow-up agreed.

Can't think of anyone? Start with categories rather than names. Draw a 2-inch circle on a piece of paper. This represents family and close friends. Who else do you know really well? Draw a larger circle around it: put in the names of any clubs or organizations you belong to. Think of courses you have attended. Who are your suppliers of professional services – how can they help? Next, draw an even larger circle to take in business contacts, past or present staff, customers, advisers, anyone who has ever helped you or you have helped. Then ask yourself – who do they know?

Try using mindmapping to extend this basic list. Or use the Lotus Blossom technique in Chapter 9 to come up with a list of potential contacts. Put one name in the centre of your first petal, and then think of eight new names or categories. Expand your eight using the full Lotus Blossom grid.

'MUST DO' LIST

☑ Base your job search on reality, not urban myths.

☑ Focus on the hidden job market.

☑ Take account of employer risk aversion in your job search strategy.

☑ Use every job-seeking strategy in the box. Combining them improves their effectiveness and shortens your job search.

☑ Keep on rethinking **You Plc** (see Exercise 13.1).

Interviews and How to Survive Them

This chapter helps you with:

∎ Getting yourself shortlisted

∎ Alternative thinking to win you the interviews

∎ Responding to job adverts

∎ Thinking the other side of the desk – the interviewer's mindset

∎ Dealing with interview anxiety

∎ Spotting buying signals

GETTING TO INTERVIEW STAGE

There are many books on interview techniques and strategies (including *Job Interviews: Top Answers to Tough Questions* by John Lees and Matthew DeLuca, McGraw-Hill, 2008). The purpose of this chapter is to show you what is going on at the heart of a recruitment interview, and to offer you a few key pointers to success.

A senior colleague once told me that getting a job offer is a matter of luck. He was right up to a point. Luck is a mixture of pure chance (the roll of the dice) and the law of averages. You can't do much about chance, but you can improve the averages. Everything you do should be aimed at improving your odds. Everything that you communicate in your **message** is intended to achieve one result: to get you a meeting. What gets you an interview? To answer that, you have to begin to see life through the eyes of a recruiter.

ALTERNATIVE THINKING TO HELP YOU TO WIN INTERVIEWS

Refuse to play by lottery rules

Negative-minded friends and fellow career changers will tell you that even getting an interview is like playing the lottery: the odds are stacked against you. In that situation, do you keep on using the same strategy in the hope that you will be lucky? Think about all the things you could do to *guarantee* that you wouldn't get in front of a decision maker: inappropriate CV, lack of preparation, and so on. What would your chances of success be? Now think of fixing just one of those things. Do the odds improve?

Get an interview through someone you know

It sounds obvious, but it's the key to success. Employers prefer to buy things they know, and that includes people. If you come even mildly recommended, your chances of a favourable decision are much higher. Being visible to a decision maker may put you in a shortlist of one.

TEN WAYS TO SHORTEN THE ODDS WHEN APPLYING TO ADVERTISED VACANCIES

You may face 200 to 1 odds of getting an interview if you apply to an advertisement. You can, however, improve the odds with these strategies:

1. Find out as much as you can about the job – Ideally by talking to someone who knows the organization well, but using *every* resource available to you, particularly the company website.

2. Make the most of initial telephone contact – If you get a chance to ask questions in advance by telephone, think about the way you present yourself and the questions you are going to ask. Don't ask questions you could discover by a fleeting glance at the website.

3. Work out the key result areas in the job – If the company doesn't say, ask. If the company doesn't know, write a draft job description and find out if it's anywhere near right.

4. Make your message clear and distinctive – The key is a short covering letter listing your relevant areas of experience and achievements as bullet points, supported by a strong CV. Think of the first page of your CV as an A4 poster offering at least half a dozen pieces of evidence that match you to the job.

5. Produce a quality CV – This sounds like kindergarten stuff, but in fact a high proportion of CVs are poorly laid out, contain errors of spelling or grammar, or miss out key information. Recruit help from a friend who knows how to lay a document out attractively on a page, using white space and different layouts for effect. Never send in a document that contains tightly packed paragraphs in a small font size. It won't be read.

6. Avoid negative messages – Don't start your covering letter 'I was made redundant in June ...' or with any other negative material. The job is hard enough without giving a recruiter reasons to reject you.

7. Prepare for screening by Human Resources – Someone in HR who may not even be working in your department could have the job of screening your application. Be clear about job titles and job reference numbers, and in your covering letter offer details that match all requirements shown as 'essential' in the job description. Pick up words and phrases used in the job advertisement: remember that applications are often read at great speed. If sending your CV by email (see Checklist J in Chapter 17) make sure your CV is in a commonly accessible format.

8. Offer a clear match to everything in the job advertisement – see the **£10 note concept** later in this chapter.

9. Think APPROPRIATE in terms of everything you present, including yourself – If you get an interview, remember that YOU are the message. What are you saying in terms of your dress, your behaviour, your history, your defensiveness when you answer questions?

10. Work out who makes the decision – Especially if the decision makor is alco going to bo your bocc tho intorvicw will givc you big clues about your future working relationship. If you haven't yet met your boss, how can you decide whether you want the job?

READING THE CLUES

When you are putting yourself forward for any kind of job, even a job that doesn't exist yet, you need to be a detective. You need to read the clues. It's sad how many people go into an interview well prepared to discuss their own virtues, but with very little idea how they will suit the job. Many plan to use the interview to find out more about the job. Don't wait that long. The clues are there in front of you in any information you can lay your hands on about the job or the organization.

Key result areas

Consider the overall **purpose** of the role and key result areas (KRAs). Why does the job exist at all? It costs an employer a great deal of money to put somebody behind a desk or out on the road: anything between 1.25 and 2 times salary (including all the real costs of hire, including recruitment, training, National Insurance and overheads). See Table 12.1 for issues that you can explore before the interview *and* during it. Recruiters will tell you that employers buy experience.

What clues does the advertisement or job profile give about past experience that an employer would like to see repeated?

Table 12.1   Asking questions about key result areas in a job

---

1. What is the purpose of the job?
Why is the job there at all? What headache, problem or opportunity does it address?

---

2. How big is the job?
Is this a big job? Does it have a lot of leverage?

---

3. How does the job fit into the organization?
How will my work depend on/affect others?

---

4. Who does the job report to?
Who takes the flak? Who is my direct boss? What is his/her boss like?

---

5. What specific skills or knowledge are required?
Will I be out of my depth? What will I need to learn quickly?

---

6. What are the main problems to be solved, and how variable (or consistent) are they?
What can go wrong? What skills will I need to fix problems? How did previous post holders survive?

---

7. What or who controls the job holder's freedom to act or make decisions?
Do I need permission for every action I take? Do I need to be a self-starter?

---

8. What end results does the job exist to achieve? How is performance measured?
What are the key results? How will they be measured?

---

9. What kind of people have done well/badly in this job in the past?
Who thrives, who survives, who sinks?

---

10. What kind of results really matter?
A probing question which you can put to the decision maker: find the right words to suit you, but try something along the lines of 'in 6 months' time you might be sitting in your garden or on a train, thinking about this appointment. How will you know if you have been successful? What will have happened or changed?'

Problems and opportunities

Where is the company going? Is it in a shrinking market and fighting its corner, or in a growth market and exploiting new opportunities? Look around for background information, using business-related search engines. Recruiters love to talk about their company's successes, and you can prompt this by knowing something about new products or services or brands in development, takeover plans or geographical growth.

Company culture

Every organization has its own personality. Some companies are naturally conservative and cautious, others dynamic. Some companies expect their employees to work long hours, others judge people by results. Many twenty-first century companies expect their employees to be up to date with this week's trends or technological advances. You will learn a lot about company culture from websites and press articles, but even more by finding someone who can tell you the inside story.

INTERVIEW PREPARATION

There is a mental and a practical side to interview preparation: thinking the right way, then doing the right things. Preparation of every kind is the key. Don't be passive when it comes to interviews: 'I'll just turn up and see what they ask me'. You wouldn't approach your bank for a loan or go into a business presentation like that. You'd prepare materials, evidence and presentation statements, you'd anticipate questions. Your career matters even more.

Avoiding interview stress

You can't. Stress is a necessary part of the process. The important thing is to use the energy that comes out of a stressful situation to your advantage, allowing it to make you more responsive, more creative. Make sure that panic doesn't lead you into a little safety corner called 'I can't do any more', which is another way of failing to anticipate and plan.

The word anxiety has its roots in 'narrowness'. When you're anxious, you put yourself in a narrow, confined space. You refuse to see openings and ways out. Narrowness is for bigots, people who want to withdraw from the bright light of creation into their shells. Stress is often the mind finding it hard to cope with possible outcomes. Look at your anxiety sideways, upside-down, whatever it takes to find something in it, paradoxically, that you enjoy (it may be excitement or uncertainty). That way you become far more open to possibilities, and to letting the process look after itself. In hindsight, most of the things you worry about in relation to jobs matter very little in the long run.

Your mindset

The prospect of hanging, said the writer Samuel Johnson, concentrates the mind wonderfully. Interviews can do the same. You can easily generate a particular mindset that shapes the whole experience, as in Figure 12.1. Next read through Table 12.2 to see how many myths you have created around job interviews, and what they are really about.

It's interesting to observe a recruitment interview and then ask the participants to say how it went. Interviewees are usually poor judges of their own performance. In an interview you suffer from information overload – there's just too much going on. The person who makes the picture dark or light is almost entirely *you*. You can look at the same questions, the same reactions, in terms of light or shadow. Is the glass half full or half empty? You can learn something from every interview experience.

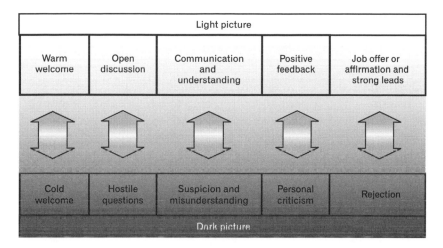

Light picture				
Warm welcome	Open discussion	Communication and understanding	Positive feedback	Job offer or affirmation and strong leads
Cold welcome	Hostile questions	Suspicion and misunderstanding	Personal criticism	Rejection
Dark picture				

Figure 12.1 Alternative ways of seeing the interview process

Table 12.2 Interviews: the essential truths

Preparation	There is no such thing as enough preparation. Do what you can, but try to do at least four times more than you think is enough.
Dress code	If you dress like a banker, you may be employed as a banker and paid a banker's salary. If you dress like a new age traveller .... Read the signals, and try to look like you're already on the payroll; it's one time in life when conformity really matters. Dump your coat with the receptionist, maybe even your briefcase – it helps to reinforce the feeling that you already work there.
Behaviour	Behaviour, like dress, sends a huge message. If you wanted to wear a sandwich board into the interview, would it say 'Employ me, I'll fit in', or 'Born to be wild. Please subsidise'? Here again, remember that selectors love to minimize risk.

Decision makers	There's little point strutting your stuff in front of someone who has no influence over the appointment decision.
Openings and closings	… should be clear and positive. Think about what you're going to say. Research suggests that interviewers are most influenced by what you say at the very beginning and very end of the interview.
Prejudice	… which simply means 'prejudging'. We all do it. If your interviewer is unreasonably prejudiced against you for some reason that has nothing to do with the job (age, skin colour, politics), do you really want to work there anyway?
CV	If your CV lets you down at interview, that's because you haven't really thought about what it's saying. It should, essentially, suggest that you are the answer to an employer's wish list. If you're using interview time to recover from CV failure, you really have set yourself an uphill battle.
Qualifications	There are probably well over 50,000 different courses and qualifications in the UK. How do employers tell one from another? On the whole, they can't. The employer who wants a 'relevant degree' may just feel flattered if surrounded by fawning graduates. Focus on the needs of the job itself in terms of experience and know-how.

The solo interview

You've heard of the Zen idea of one hand clapping? Let me introduce to you the concept of interviewer-free interviewing.

Find time, on your own, to reflect on the interview. Think of it as a time management exercise: a short window of opportunity for you to impress. Look at the requirements of the job, known or guessed. Now have a conversation with the best part of yourself, not the negative voice that's whispering 'You can't *do* this!', but your better half, the one that's prepared to have a go. The solo interview both anticipates questions and places the job within a much larger pattern. You'll know what the big questions are, but Table 12.3 offers some prompts.

Table 12.3 Questions to prompt your interview preparation

- What in my past makes me a good choice?

- How would this job be a great opportunity to use my skills/experience/gifts?

- How would this job be a good stepping stone?

- How does it fit into my life plan?

- Who will I help if I do this job?

- How does this job/company fit my personal and work values?

- Since employers buy experience, which parts of my past are going to be in my window display?

- Which of my past achievements are most relevant here?

- What presentation statements do I need to rehearse/improve?

- Why do I want this job?

- What problems will I solve in the job?

- What special combination of skills do I have that no-one else can offer?

- What will it *feel* like to do this job? In the first week? The first month? After a year?

- How will I know if I am successful?

- Which parts of the job will be really me?

- Will this job make me happier than I am now? How would others tell?

SHINING AT THE INTERVIEW

At Interview, be yourself, but the best half of yourself.

John Courtis

What on earth are they going to ask?

Prepare well, do your homework about the organization and the job, plan for interview questions, and you can shine at interview. Others will be trying to 'wing it' without thinking the activity through. Begin by putting yourself on the other side of the desk and adopting the interviewer's point of view. Starting with the key result areas of the job, what questions are almost certain to come up?

See the **Key Checklists** in Chapter 17 for more details of difficult interview questions, and see the relevant chapters in *Job Interviews: Top Answers to Tough Questions* and *Why You? – CV Messages to Win Jobs*.

Questions focused on skills

Supply *evidence* of your skills. Even relatively sophisticated competence-based interviews are essentially saying 'You say you have skill X. Tell me when you used this skill successfully.' Work out the skills that will make a real difference to the job, and match them to the skills that you know you exercise with ease and enthusiasm.

The £10 note concept

No, this isn't advice on bribery and corruption, but a way of getting you to read the clues. Think of the job as a £10 note torn in half:

Look at that ragged edge where the bank note has been torn. That's what the job should look like to you: a series of connections. Each connection is a clue to the way a post holder might be successful, a piece of information about a key result area.

Now think of yourself as the other half of that bank note. That's the mental image you should have in mind, so you can communicate this to the employer, and everything you do in the interview should be saying, for example, 'I understand that you need problem-solving skills. I'm good at coming up with solutions to problems under pressure. This is when I did it.'

Minimum qualifications

Employers are clear about the qualifications they *think* they need for the job. How far are these requirements justified by the job itself? How many are there just to filter out candidates, or to massage a manager's ego? If you lack the named qualifications, demonstrate how your experience compensates, and is maybe even more up to date or relevant than paper qualifications. As with any apparent hurdle: address the problem directly, don't avoid it.

Your weak points

How will you cope in a crisis or under pressure? It's difficult for an interviewer to gauge this at interview. Some will try to put you under stress during the interview. Better interviewers will ask you about times in the past when you overcame challenges while working to strict deadlines, or times when everything went wrong and you found some way of coping.

Interpreting interview language

Listen for verbal clues: the snippets of information the interviewer gives you about the job, the questions that are asked – all these things give you huge clues about the job, but also about the language you should use. If the questions are all about targets and performance, match your language.

Listen for checklists

Be aware of the structure of an interview. Some interviewers want to jump straight in with a question of the 'Tell me about yourself' variety (technically, a high-order, open question). Others will have a game of two halves in mind: a first half where they go through a checklist of the things they want to know, and a second half where they probe things more deeply and get a chance to discover some background. If you sense a 'checklist' approach, don't go into too much detail with each answer, since it irritates the interviewer. You can always give a brief answer and then offer more detail if invited.

Hiring winners

Employers are geared to a continuous process of success. So naturally they want to hire winners. Recruiting organizations are happy to talk about potential, but the primary question is:

'Where's the evidence of past achievement?' Essentially what a recruiting employer is looking for is a win/win: both parties get something good out of the deal. Once an employer has decided you are the one, then an interview turns much more into a negotiation: 'If I offer you X, then you will achieve Y ...'.

Looking at the big picture, recruiters are likely to spot winners by asking questions that all fit, ultimately, within a six-point structure, as shown in Table 12.4.

Table 12.4   The six-point structure at the heart of all interview questions

1. **What brought you to us?** Why did you apply? What is your career plan?
2. **What do you have to offer?** What do you bring to the party? What solutions do you have to offer which match our problems?
3. **How well do you understand us?** Have you worked out how we tick as an organization? Have you worked out the key result areas of the job?
4. **Who are you?** What kind of person are you? Are you like us? Will you fit in? What will you add to a team?
5. **Why *you*?** – rather than someone else with the same general profile? What puts you ahead of the pack? What's your unique selling point?
6. **What will it take to bring you on board?** What will you cost us? How do we have to motivate and develop you to retain you in the future?

COMPETENCY-BASED SELECTION PROCEDURES

Currently employers are eager to measure competencies as well as skills. A 'competency' is in fact a combination of know-how, skills, attitude and demonstrated behaviours – all directed towards outcomes which actively assist an employer.

A competency is not just about what you do, but how you do it, and to what level.

Prepare by looking carefully at any information you can find about competencies which are considered essential or useful for the job. You may be given a written statement listing the competencies and inviting you to give detailed information about times when you have used them. Alternatively, you may have to make an educated guess (from the job description and information about the organization) at the five or six top competencies for the role.

A strategy used by a number of employers now is to give you a list of up to 20 competencies, and to ask you to write a written statement against each one. If you do so, look back on this information carefully when you plan your interview performance. Ideally, have one or two ideas up your sleeve of things that you have not mentioned in writing.

If you are not asked for written evidence, don't make the mistake of thinking that competency-based questions won't come up. They will usually be flagged by the introductory words 'Tell me about a time when …'. Look at what you believe to be the main competencies required by the role and plan short, upbeat examples of what you have actually done, and when, and what the end results were.

THE FINISHING LINE – THE END OF THE INTERVIEW

Timeframe

Listen for a change of tense. Most interviews begin by looking at your past. Indeed, some careers counsellors say that's exactly the problem with a CV – it's a historical document. If that's all it is, then it's an **obituary**. It only talks about your past. To address the needs of the job, address the future. Try to encourage the employer to see you in the job. Suggest ideas and possibilities for the company: it weaves you into the fabric of the company's future.

Buying signals

We all demonstrate buying signals, and some people are trained to spot them. If a market trader is trying to sell you something, he watches your buying signals carefully: you might try a garment on for size, explain its virtues to a friend or check how much cash is in your wallet. A less obvious buying signal is that you ask questions about the product: Is there a guarantee? How long will the battery last? Interest is a powerful buying signal.

The first, but perhaps least obvious, buying signal in an interview is when the interviewer starts to talk about the present, and then the future. Stay with that, encourage it. The stronger the image in the interviewer's mind of you sitting in a real office at a real desk, the greater the chance it will become reality.

Other buying signals? An obvious one is when the interview turns to point 6 in Table 12.4: how much will you cost? No one discusses terms unless they are interested. This is *not* the time to say how little you would settle for. Bring the discussion back to key result areas, to the value you can add to the organization. Ask the employer what he had in mind when he decided to advertise the vacancy or start seeing people. Only as a last resort should you mention what you are actually looking for, because you're in danger of setting far too low a limit. If you absolutely have to mention a figure, base it on hard knowledge of what others in similar positions are earning, or aspire to, and then add a bit. Remember that employers are buyers, and buyers always feel happier if they can knock you down from your initial price.

Never, ever, fall into the trap of answering the question 'How much do you need?' You should aim to be paid what you are worth to an employing organization, in relation to the value you add, the professionalism you deliver and the size of the problems you can solve. The final factor is what the market will bear, but at this stage of the process – at this stage only – you have the upper hand. They want you. They are falling in love with you. And just for a fleeting moment you have some leverage.

Closing with enthusiasm

The first and last things you say at interview will probably be remembered more than anything else you say, so think particularly about what you say as the interview closes. Always have some good, detailed questions you can ask about the job and the organization (see below). This might be a time to get across one or two key messages (see Exercise 12.2). You might also ask for the job. Failing that, the question 'is there anything else I need to tell you that would help you come to an appointment decision?' might take the employer into buying mode.

Questions *you* should ask as the interview closes

When asked 'do you have any questions for us?' too many candidates politely say 'no, you've covered everything in great detail, thank you'. Wrong answer! Say this, and the interviewer feels you have little real interest in the job. Questions will arise from the interview, but prepare three or four good ones in advance. Good ones come in two types: questions that show that you have thought carefully about the key result areas of the job, and questions that help the interviewer to picture you in the post. The main thing is to show interest and enthusiasm. Before you ask any questions at the end of the interview, **say something positive** about the role. Then your question sounds like *your* buying signal: you like the job so much you want to know more.

You won't get the chance to ask more than a couple of questions at the end of an interview. If one or two pop up during the meeting, take your cue from the interviewer as to the topic. Your main chance is, however, at the end, and the main purpose of your questions is message reinforcement, not information gathering. You want to leave a final positive impression about your awareness of the role and your strong interest in it. You can decide later whether you want the job; for now, make only positive noises.

A couple of danger areas remain. Avoid asking questions about selection criteria: they so often sound as if you are asking for special treatment or believe that the interviewer doesn't know what he's doing. And don't ask anything you could have discovered by spending 5 minutes looking at the company website.

REJECTION

It's trite to say that you shouldn't feel 'rejected' if turned down by an employer. Recover in your own time, and try not to take it personally: people are rejected for all kinds of arbitrary reasons. In any job search you will receive more rejections than acceptances. This is a neutral statistical fact. Be careful not to use it as evidence to support 'Yes, but' thinking: 'I knew I was unemployable ...'.

INTERVIEWS WITH RECRUITMENT CONSULTANTS

Recruitment consultants are, of course, professional selectors who make a living finding workers to fill particular vacancies for client employers. Remember that the recruitment consultant will not make the final selection decision, but is a gatekeeper between you and the decision maker. You are dealing with an **intermediary**, i.e. someone who is both a broker and barrier. If a recruitment consultant is talking to you, it is likely to be for a particular post. Few recruiters will give you an interview otherwise, unless they are hungry for information about your market sector. Some pointers:

▋ The consultant acts as the employer's eyes and ears, but will see things in an even sharper perspective: if there's something unacceptable about your dress code, interview behaviour, CV or qualifications, the consultant will be highly attuned to it. The reason is simple: a recruitment consultant wants to put forward a **safe bet**.

▋ Therefore, you need to know what buttons you are pressing in terms of safety, reliability or energy and enthusiasm. Get the recruiter to describe to you what he or she is really looking for, and respond to that.

▋ Finally, it really pays to encourage your consultant to switch from gatekeeper to lifelong friend. Ask for professional advice on your interview technique or the state of the market. Be flexible and available. Don't let your doubts about recruitment consultancies or agencies influence this one interview or decision. Agencies need a flow of enthusiastic, committed candidates. Just as you will show an employer how your presence in the workplace will solve problems, be a problem solver to any intermediaries.

EXERCISE 12.1 – TEMPORARY TERRORISM

Just for a few moments, imagine the worst. You face an interviewer with a huge overdraft and an even bigger headache. She's having a bad day, and will look at everything you have put forward in a bad light. Be that person just for a few moments. What's the worst question you could ask yourself, knowing your own weaknesses? What's the second worst question? What areas of preparation are you weakest on? Where do you think your skills are inadequate? Where do you lack evidence of achievement?

Prepare for that interview, and the real one will be a dream. But now it's vital to remember how easy it was to see the whole thing negatively. Why is it that you are happier seeing the interview as a nightmare? Why are you more prepared to believe a poor self-image than a positive one? If it's all about the colour you paint the scene in advance, what happens if you tell yourself how brilliant you will be? Sounds corny, but try it. Self-confidence is just as powerful a career change tool as skills, experience or knowledge.

EXERCISE 12.2 – SHOPPING LIST

Find a vacancy that interests you, perhaps through a published advertisement. Ring or write for a job description.

Take an A4 piece of paper and divide it into two vertical columns. Interrogating the job description, write out the employer's **shopping list**, everything the recruiter is looking for, using the following checklist:

■ List all the 'wanted' elements: qualifications, experience, know-how, etc.

■ Work out what's essential, and what's desirable.

■ Now use your own industry knowledge to work out all the stuff between the lines: the unstated assumptions.

■ Finally, try to think yourself in the interviewer's shoes. If you were interviewing, what would you really be looking for? What achievements would you recognize?

Now, in the right-hand column, write in your matching claims *and* evidence. Think in both terms – you should be able to say what you can do, and give an example of an achievement that substantiates your claim. Go back to skill clips and presentation statements in Chapter 7.

EXERCISE 12.3 – THE POLITICIAN'S TRICK

Listen to a seasoned politician being interviewed on the radio. One thing you may notice is that, no matter what questions are asked, the minister always manages to make three or four strong points about government policy. The questions just provide an opportunity: the airtime is being used as a way of getting a particular message across.

You can use the same technique. **Step 1**: look at the *key result areas* in a job, and ask yourself 'What *three points* is it vital that I make during this interview?' **Step 2**: write them down, and rehearse a clear, concise way of talking about them. **Step 3**: make sure you get those three points across at interview. Why three points? Politicians know that their listeners can only hold a few ideas in mind at one time. Interviewers are much the same.

'MUST DO' LIST:

☑ Practise being a detective, picking up vital clues about the employer's needs.

☑ Don't go to any interview without exploring the purpose of the job, and key result areas.

☑ Think of yourself as a product which solves the employer's problems.

☑ Learn how to spot buying signals during the interview.

☑ Try anticipating an employer's risk aversion in your interview preparation.

☑ What strategies are you going to use to ensure that at interview you are *the best you there is*?

☑ Prepare for the worst and best interview questions. See *Job Interviews: Top Answers To Tough Questions* by John Lees and Matthew Deluca (McGraw-Hill, 2008).

☑ Use the interview checklists in Chapter 17.

How to Love the Job You've Got

This chapter looks at ways to:

▪ Learn to use tools from your career transition to apply to the rest of your life

▪ Acquire job survival skills

▪ Turn your next job into a success

▪ Manage and negotiate your future

Furious activity is no substitute for understanding.

H. H. Williams

CHANGING THE WAY YOU THINK OF YOUR CAREER

Most of us have inherited a strong idea of a career. We think of it as progression up a ladder of growth and success. This model has been put under considerable pressure in the past 25 years.

Few people now have a 'job for life'. Where our parents' generation enjoyed high job security in return for company loyalty, workers of the twenty-first century work under a 'psychological contract' under which employers do not guarantee employment, and employees have to take responsibility for their own career development and to secure their own employability.

The process is about positive goal setting, and about changing the way you think about your experience and your career as a whole.

This chapter introduces you to the idea of managing your career, but for a great deal more information see *Take Control of Your Career* (McGraw-Hill, 2006).

What is career management?

All too often we think that career management is about having a career *plan*: a clear timetable for how you will move from one rung of the ladder to the next. So many career changers believe 'I am the only person in the world who doesn't have a career plan'. In fact, very few people have their lives planned out that precisely. We usually start with a problem such as 'I need a job' or 'I hate my job' and then look around for some kind of action. Most career 'plans' look something like Figure 13.1.

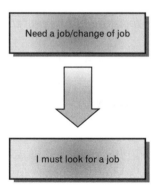

Figure 13.1 A conventional career strategy

This is the way we are taught to fix life problems, by using A–Z thinking: I have a problem, I fix the problem. This is why so many of us make a job change driven by the first job that comes along, almost as if you are going to plan a holiday by picking on the first flight you find on a departures board at the airport.

A great strategy for a spontaneous adventure, but perhaps not the best way of deciding how to spend most of your waking life.

The difficulty is that we don't fix the problem, we fix the symptoms. And sometimes this means that people actually take their problem with them. Anyone who is seriously thinking 'I need to change jobs' should ask themselves 'can I fix the job I've got?' We need to look at ideas before making decisions, research before job search.

Should I have a career plan?

I have come to believe that career management isn't about having a step-by-step plan for your whole life. It's more about being able to respond to the here and now: to recognize the opportunities that life offers.

The problem is that we use the idea 'I should plan my career' as a way of avoiding the issue. It seems too big a project. Naturally we also beat ourselves up for not doing it. As Chapter 1 shows, we have no difficulty at all finding reasons not to have a great career. And so it follows that we will find any avoidance strategy to avoid a career review. Why? Maybe because you'll have to ask yourself difficult questions. Maybe because you instinctively know that something needs changing, and a review will require activity. Avoidance strategies usually come out of a reluctance to change, even if this means moving from an uncomfortable position. The status quo is very attractive, and you will even adopt a language that locks you into it: *Don't rock the boat ... Better the devil you know ... The grass is always greener ....*

At least begin by looking at your major areas of dissatisfaction, and allow yourself to imagine (without any commitment) what is possible to fix where you are. Sometimes this might mean changing the rules, using some lateral thinking or surprising your boss with a radical thought. But aren't these the skills that your employer expects you to use anyway?

CONDUCTING YOUR OWN CAREER REVIEW

Here are some pointers to conducting a career review for yourself. This takes time, a little imagination and some fairly robust strategies to cope with 'Yes, but' thinking.

Past performance

Look at your work history. Understand and accept what has happened in your past. You don't have to repeat mistakes or experiences. Use the tools contained in this book to assess all the things you have to offer: your know-how, your skills, your achievements, your attitude to work. Focus on your strengths, and work out your wish list of how you'd like your job to be.

Where are you now?

Look at your current job as objectively as you can. What's the real problem? What are the opportunities? If push comes to shove, what can you *really* change? Review your progress and update your 'message' every 3 months. This means keeping a personal portfolio of work you have done, problems you have overcome, where you have added value to your organization and made a difference. This will provide the basis for you to assess your skills, achievements, development needs and future opportunities. It will also enable you to know your true worth and marketability.

Self-review regularly: at least once a year, fill one side of A4 with a review of

▌ your progress this year

▌ your main achievements

▌ how you think your boss sees you

▌ your learning plan

▌ how you are stocking your lifeboat in case this ship sinks.

Improve your offer

Learn new skills or become more proficient at old ones. Read widely and keep up to date with the changing environment and both the demands and opportunities it creates. Don't restrict networking and informational interviews to times when you are undertaking job search. Seek out people who can give you cutting-edge ideas, tell you about interesting projects and keep you informed about industry developments.

Don't get so bogged down in your job that you miss learning opportunities. Make sure you go to conferences and exhibitions and industry seminars, even if this is in your own time.

Communicate your achievements

Make your successes known. This doesn't mean point-scoring or bragging, but making sure that key people know how you have added value to the organization. Be willing to share information about *how* you achieved your results so that others can learn from you. Understand what is expected from you, by whom and when. Remember that if your boss changes, then the expectations are likely to change too. Your attitude towards change will say much about you, especially when others are fighting against it.

Be ready, almost at the drop of a hat, to communicate:

■ your key successes this year

■ your top motivated skills and preferred working contexts

■ at least three suggestions of ways you could work more effectively and create new opportunities for your employer.

Become 'politically aware'

Organizational survivors are often not those with the best skills, but those who are most keenly tuned to office politics. Make sure you are seen as an innovator, as a key player, not as dead wood. Understand what your boss really wants in life, and help to provide it. Be very careful around new bosses: re-establish your presence just as if you were starting a new job.

Look for win/win

We work to become, not to acquire.

Elbert G. Hubbard

Planning ahead doesn't mean knowing all the moves, but is about having a set of personal objectives: a wish list. This will relate to the skills you want to use and develop, your learning, and the scope and size of your job. Organizations find it diffi-cult to interpret personal wish lists until they are communi-cated in terms that are attractive: your offer. Show how both parties gain: win/win. But don't assume that the employer sees a win just because you do. Good salespeople will tell you that win/win really means 'This is how *I* see that *I* win/This is how *you* see that *you* win'.

Rethink appraisals

Try the **suggestion box** concept. This doesn't mean the traditional box in the works canteen which gets a half-baked idea once in a blue moon. It's about encouraging both parties to come to an appraisal meeting with positive suggestions. Individuals should be encouraged to come to a meeting at least every 6 months with statements such as 'Here is an opportunity I have identified that draws on my top skills … I will benefit because … You will benefit because …'.

Managers get worn down by conventional appraisals because they are faced with problems that they find very difficult to solve. If you go into an appraisal with a positive offer couched in win/win language, it's much more difficult for an employer to say 'no'. And a real win/win is that you can encourage your boss to rethink what appraisals are all about.

Employers often say 'but what if the employee wants something I can't offer?' My reply is always: 'Then you've just received early warning of a retention problem.' At least 50% of the time it makes good economic sense to redesign the job of a key player rather than lose her. These are facts to keep up your sleeve when negotiating your future.

Watch out for panic signals

It's surprising how quickly people move from moderate satisfaction to 'I hate this job'. It's equally surprising how often a client who tells me 'I need to be out of this job today' can switch to a feeling that the job can be fixed from the inside. However, we can outgrow jobs. It's no bad thing to leave an organization when you have done as much as you can do in a job.

One other key point about retention: research data show that people leave managers, not organizations. Ask yourself: is it the job, the organization or the person? And the next question has to be 'What can I fix?' You may find that your organization is happy to change your job or transfer you to a new manager. You may be more of an asset than the person making your life miserable.

Act positive

Acting positively isn't about walking round with a fixed grin, flattering the boss or supporting junk ideas. But it does mean that people in your team should think about you as the kind of person who will give things a go, take on board new ideas or go the extra mile. You don't have to undergo a personality transplant: just listen for all of those 'Yes, but' ideas, and don't act on them. Be willing to look at new ideas, and don't get caught up in a culture of office cynicism. It's all too easy to say 'It'll never work', and easier still to act on it.

Being positive doesn't mean being a doormat, either: have your own agenda, and put forward ideas that will work for you as well as for your organization.

NEGOTIATE YOUR FUTURE

The early twenty-first century is an odd time to be in work. It's a time of major redundancies and stock market uncertainty, but also huge skill shortages and retention problems.

Use the 'You Plc' exercise at the end of this chapter to work out the value that you currently offer your employer, and how you can adapt or improve in the future.

When job seeking you should only negotiate pay when the employer has decided he or she can't live without you. Similarly the best time to renegotiate your salary is when your employer is most aware of your 'offer', most aware of the value you bring to an organization. See Figure 13.2 for tips.

DON'T be tempted to talk about what you 'need'. Talk about the value you add.

DON'T jump in with a figure too soon. Spell out your 'offer' first.

DON'T guess on what the job is worth. Find out the upper and lower points of the salary typically paid for this kind of job. Rehearse all the reasons why you should be paid in the top 25% of this band.

DON'T hold a gun to your employer's head like 'I am getting offers from …' or 'I'll be forced to look for another job'. Do that and you have no offer, just a threat.

DON'T focus just on the past: describe what you can do in the future.
....

DO focus on what you are bringing to the deal, remembering to explain in 'win' language which means something to your employer.

DO – if the employer won't move on the money – ask for an early review date, or an enhanced bonus, or some other way of improving the package quickly.

DO look at alternatives. If you can't get a pay rise, can you use your position of leverage to make the job more interesting?

DO negotiate like a pro. Remember the 'salami' technique. Work out the difference between what you want and what the employer will offer. Divide it by 12, then say 'We're talking about a difference of £XX per month. You must pay more than that in photocopying/coffee/stamps …'.

DO look, act and sound like a person already doing the job you want to be promoted into.

Figure 13.2 Tips on getting a pay rise or promotion

EXERCISE 13.1 – 'YOU PLC' IN 8 STEPS

When you are marketing yourself to employers, it's sometimes useful to think of yourself as a one-person corporation: 'You Plc'. This is an idea championed in William Bridges' famous book *Creating You & Co.*, and adapted here as a tool for helping you to undertake your own career review. Take a blank piece of paper. Look at what sets you ahead of the competition by answering these questions:

1. What is the **main** service you provide to your current organization (e.g. problem solving, contributing new ideas, coaching, managing relationships)?

2. How does this activity match the needs of the organization?

3. What results have you achieved?

4. What do you have to offer which is a better solution to your organization's needs than similar services from other people? (Think of other potential suppliers, internal or external.)

5. What do you think is the main service you have to offer your own or another organization in **future**?

6. How can you improve, update and communicate your offer more effectively?

7. What new results do you think you can achieve?

8. Why do you think that your future service will be a better solution for an organization's needs than others can provide? (Again, include both internal and external suppliers.)

EXERCISE 13.2 – TIME BALANCE

How would you like your time to be balanced in your ideal job?

Using Table 13.1, consider your present job and your ideal job.

Table 13.1 Time balance

In the left column write down a percentage score for each activity in your **present job**. Then do the same thing for your **ideal job** in the right column.

Present job		Ideal job
	Working on my own Reflecting, thinking, working things out, being given space to sort out a problem or finish a piece of work, writing something, being given time to be myself.	
	Working one-to-one Explaining, persuading, influencing, selling, coaching, managing, teaching, etc.	
	Working in a small team Meeting informally or formally, having discussions or debates, problem solving, planning, sharing or brainstorming ideas, reviewing, getting things done, etc.	
	Extending your network Telephoning new contacts, networking, meeting plenty of new people, going to conferences, seminars, etc.	
	Working with an audience Public speaking, performing, entertaining, giving talks, informing larger groups, running training courses, etc.	
	Other Define this yourself:	
100%	**Total**	100%

'MUST DO' LIST

☑ Prepare yourself to take control of your career, because no-one else will.

☑ Decide now how you can remotivate yourself to undertake a personal career review regularly.

☑ Find a coach or mentor. If your employer doesn't offer one, recruit your own – even if it's just to look at problems and help you to suggest solutions.

☑ Start a file or notebook to record activities, achievements and contacts. Make the first sheet your wish list of how you would like your work to be.

☑ Make a diary date 3 months ahead to update your review.

☑ Look at your life/work balance. What are your priorities? What would you like to change?

For further discussion on

■ planning your career

■ avoiding career traps and career limiting actions

■ renegotiating your job

■ understanding the way your organization sees you

■ rethinking your life/work balance

see John Lees' *Take Control of Your Career* (McGraw-Hill, 2006)

Building a Portfolio Career

This chapter looks at:

▌ Continuous change: refreshing your career

▌ New choices in working arrangements

▌ Temporary, interim and flexible working arrangements

▌ Building a portfolio career

Built to last now means built to change.
                                    Stan Davis and Christopher Meyer

CAREER REFRESHMENT

This is a book that acknowledges the importance of work. Finding the right kind of work can feed you. However, the job you love now may not be a job you want to do forever. Our motivations for work and our sense of the rewards we get out of it change as we grow older. Careers need refreshing from time to time. We are becoming increasingly attuned to the idea that we will probably change career paths several times during a working lifetime. In other words, your long-term focus may not just be on getting a job you'll love, but on getting a series of jobs you'll love, and perhaps doing some of those jobs at the same time.

Things to come

Charles Handy predicted that in the twenty-first century more than 50% of jobs would be something other than 'proper' full-time jobs: part-time, flexi-hours, fixed-term contract, temporary, self-employed or some other variation. He hasn't got it far wrong. There has been huge attention to flexible working, which of course means different things to employers and workers. You may want to leave work early to go to a night class, or bank flexitime so you can regularly take long week-ends. Your employer might want you to be part of the 24/7 economy.

It's something of a cliché to say that work is changing fast. The key question is how we anticipate these changes, and how we make sense of them. One of the strongest ways of flexing in response to the marketplace is to rethink the nature of work itself, and to become increasingly open to the idea of becoming a portfolio worker.

PORTFOLIO CAREERS

Pipe dream or possibility?

You may have heard of the 'portfolio' career, but what is it, and does it really exist? The answer is an unequivocal 'yes'. The term is used to describe a deliberate choice, mixing and matching different kinds of work to find the ideal balance, which will be about time, flexibility and travel, but also about the kind of work you do. A marketing specialist works for 2 days a week at corporate rates, subsiding her work as a lecturer. Some hold down three or four appointments simultaneously; for example, an HR consultant who also works as a board member of a health trust, a non-executive director of a publishing company and a charity trustee.

One driving factor here is the decline of the well-funded company pension scheme, a feature of the late twentieth century marketplace that encouraged both long service and early retirement. Problems in funding such schemes mean that many of us have to work longer to fund our retirement, but as we become increasingly more responsible for our own pension fund, there is also less pressure for people to stick to traditional working models. If it seems likely that we will have to work longer into old age, then we may want to prepare for the journey ahead by thinking about the kind of skills we would like to use.

Is portfolio working a middle-aged luxury?

It may be true that portfolio careers are available largely to older workers. This is partly because it's more important for younger people to establish a track record in permanent work, and possibly because older workers have sometimes resolved financial needs or moved beyond them. However, repeated surveys point to the growth of self-employment, and this means that increasingly we are getting used to the idea of not having a regular pay cheque. Financial security, of course, is a factor, simply because you can cope with a variable income. However, if your income has always been variable, adding different kinds of work to the mix is far from threatening. So we have the self-employed joiner who also buys and sells antiques, the part-time HR specialist who works as a freelance book editor, and the lecturer who runs her own business as an equal opportunities trainer. Even though few of these people would automatically recognize themselves as 'portfolio workers', they are living examples of a new, pragmatic and highly inventive method of working.

What kind of people benefit from this new working method? People who enjoy variety and change. People who become dispirited by the constraints of a conventional career, which may mean doing the same thing for ever. People of all ages who want to take more control over the way they spend their working week, but who wisely want to mix conventional and free-thinking methods, predictable income streams with creative possibilities. One of the exciting things about portfolio work is that it maintains an air of unpredictability: you never know what kind of project or enquiry is coming in next, and you may be doing an entirely different mix of work in 12 months' time.

Be aware, however, that society rarely offers you these opportunities on a plate. You also need to think about how you will communicate this job mix if you are applying for a full-time permanent position at some time in the future. Having said that, portfolio careers often offer a high degree of work satisfaction simply because you are managing your time so that you spend more of it doing a job you love.

'Yes, but' thinking (again)

Your friends and colleagues may not immediately recognize what you are trying to do, and wonder why you aren't applying for a 'proper' job. They may tell you that you are 'playing' at work or operating on the edge of the 'real world', ignoring the fact that many of your colleagues and friends are already doing the same thing. One of the great advantages of portfolio work is that you are in a very strong position to introduce new services and strategies as the market changes, and you're far less at the whim of a single organization. After several years of corporate downsizing, this degree of control may make all the difference.

You will need to draw heavily on two of the major themes of this book. The first is to dig deep in terms of creative approaches: what could you actually do? What kinds of work could you mix? The second is that you will have to work hard at communicating what you do: explaining your distinctive work mix, and actively seeking out people who can help you to find customers and other kinds of contact. Ultimately, if you plan it right, the work will find you, but that means you have to invest a great deal of time and energy initially into making a great range of contacts (see Chapter 11 for more tips on networking).

PATHWAYS TOWARDS THE PORTFOLIO CAREER

You may already be on your way to a multidimensional career because you have already started to explore some of the unconventional methods of working that are now available. These are set out below, along with the typical advantages and disadvantages experienced by workers who have tried them.

Temporary or contract work

Temporary work is often provided by recruitment agencies, and there seems to be no field of work where temps are not engaged, from van driving to financial management. It's best if you can take temporary work for a positive reason: seek opportunities that will expand your knowledge or skills, or extend your range of contacts. Be aware that there is a high chance of being retained in a permanent job just because you are already a known quantity. However, do be careful that agencies don't have a narrow picture of what you can do. They will assume that you will want to do what you have done in the past. Seek refreshment by asking for different kinds of work assignment. When you are in the temporary role, try to negotiate access to the learning opportunities and new contacts that are on offer to your permanent colleagues.

For: You can quickly acquire new skills and a wide range of work experience. This is often a good way of gaining experience in new fields of work.

Against: You may not get access to training and career development opportunities. It's also a difficult route if you want to change careers, as temping agencies are all too keen to pigeon-hole you.

Interim

Interim work is essentially a form of short-term contract for more experienced managers. These roles are typically filled by senior staff with experience of managing companies or functions. An employer hires them in to cover a staff shortage or, more likely, to deal with a particular project or workload. Interim assignments can last for anything from 2 weeks to 2 years, but it's more common that a company is seeking professional expertise over something like a 3–6 month period. Unlike a consultant, your role is not just to make recommendations, but to implement them. There is now a wide range of interim management consultancies in the UK, and if you are thinking of working in this field, investigate what they have to offer. However, the best course of action is to talk to someone who is currently undertaking an interim assignment. Remember, too, that your most likely source of interim work is with an employer you already know.

For: Allows you to gain experience of new work cultures without getting locked in to the company payroll.

Against: You have to consider this as a career step rather than a fill-in move, since you may need to devote considerable energy to securing your next move while you are currently working in your present one. You may also have to work some distance away from home.

Part-time or flexitime

You may want to choose part-time or flexible working hours for a variety of reasons: family responsibilities, easing the pain of daily travel, or perhaps because you are allowing yourself time and energy to do something else with your life (learning a new skill, taking a qualification, starting up a fledgling business ...). Remember that a great many part-time jobs are negotiated rather than advertised. Employers find it difficult to attract candidates to part-time positions, so they are often filled by word of mouth. Alternatively, a job that is first conceived as a full-time position may be renegotiated as a part-time position or job share (see below).

For: Helps to preserve energy for some of the other things you want to do in life, which may include other portfolio jobs.

Against: You will probably put in more hours than you are paid for, and you may be underexposed in the company and so not have a sufficiently high profile with decision makers, and so fail to gain career development opportunities.

Job sharing

With the rise in flexible working, a great many employers have become tuned in to the idea of a job share. This has some benefits for organizations (two people tend to put in slightly more overall effort than one) and clear benefits for candidates who only want to work certain hours or on certain days of the week. A parent staying at home 2 days a week, for example, can save significantly on child-care costs.

If you want to take an active strategy rather than hoping that something will come along, it's a good idea to find someone else to be your job-share partner, and make a joint application for a job. You may have to explain what a job share is and how it works (so take the time to interview someone who is already working in a job share), but many employers who have equal opportunities policies will take your application seriously, and you may be providing a creative solution to their problem.

For: A good stepping stone towards portfolio working.

Against: It is often difficult to persuade an employer to agree to a job share unless you (and your job-share colleague) are already working for the organization.

Short-term or fixed-term arrangements

Employers offer short-term or fixed-term contracts for various reasons, but usually the intention is to control payroll costs. However, many people hired on short-term contracts are retained in permanent roles (employers prefer to hire staff they already know – see Chapter 11).

For: Ensures you keep your offer fresh and clear to your employer.

Against: Uncertainty towards the end of your contract.

Mixed mode: employed and self-employed

At the end of the tax year many people complete tax returns which record their income both from PAYE employment and from self-employed activities. They may work as a part-time lecturer or writer, or possibly they obtain an income from renovating furniture or making hand-made clothes. They may have more than one employer. They may have an income from renting out a second property. You don't have to be restricted by either/or thinking. Investigate alternative careers by trying out something different one day a week or at a weekend. Others start businesses on a part-time basis, phasing one kind of work in and another out as a business starts to become successful.

For: This really is often the first step towards portfolio working.

Against: You may have to invest in your own training costs or overheads, so you may incur costs and suffer a variable income during the initial phase.

Negotiating the right working arrangement for you

Don't begin by giving an employer a reason to exclude you from the recruitment process. If you start by saying 'I am only interested in a job that is part-time/interim/short-term ...' you are giving a recruiter a reason to end the conversation.

The golden rule is to begin with the needs of the organization, not your working restrictions. In other words, find out what the employer needs, get them to realize what you have to offer, and if you are both happy with the result you may have the opportunity to negotiate something different. Some employers would rather have the right person on a part-time basis than not have anyone at all. Others may be attracted by your idea of doing the job on a consultancy basis. If they want you, things become negotiable, including working conditions. There are, of course, exceptions, particularly with highly structured organizations. Even local authorities, however, are positive if approached by a job-share 'couple' (see Job Sharing above).

One-step-at-a-time career breakthrough

Many career and self-help books are written around the idea that we all have a hidden, 'real' self, and if we can unlock this secret then the answer to the question 'what should I do with my life?' will become crystal clear. The popular press reinforces the idea that deep down we all have a single dream job, and what we long for is an overnight transformation. That's why newspapers love stories of 'accountant becomes skydiver' or 'commando becomes nanny'.

In fact, such transformations are relatively rare. It's far more common that people progress by gradual steps and 'try on' different careers. Many of us do this quite naturally in our first 10 years of work, when it's relatively easy to change direction and experiment. We often write off this period of our life as uncertain 'drifting'.

Making a huge leap in your career is not straightforward. This is particularly true if this involves a change of field (e.g. moving from marketing to photography) or a major change of lifestyle (e.g. from financial director to author). It's a risky process because it's about moving from known to unknown.

And others will be only too keen to tell you how risky your idea is.

CAREER BREAKTHROUGH BY INCREMENTS

- Don't think just in terms of a single job you'll love. Think of career pathways, clusters, patterns, etc.

- Be better informed about key changes in the way people work, and the impact of new technology and new working methods.

- Think again about what you recognize as a career and a 'proper' job.

- Investigate the different routes others have taken towards portfolio careers.

- Talk to people who have made the journey before you. Talk to people who have successfully reinvented the work they do. Use the REVEAL method of informational interviews (see Appendix 1).

- Ignore the job myths. Find out for yourself.

- Weigh up the real pros and cons of change. How can you minimize the risk and maximize your return?

- Watch out (here as much as anywhere) for the overwhelming, crippling power of 'Yes, but' thinking.

- Unsure whether self-employment would suit you? Try the Autonomy Audit at www.johnleescareers.com

- Look at the balance between passive and active. For more strategies for steering your own course see John Lees' *Take Control of Your Career* (McGraw-Hill, 2006).

'MUST DO' LIST:

- ☑ Describe your ideal portfolio career. Write down what you would be doing during a typical month.

- ☑ Focus on the steps you would need to take to make it happen.

- ☑ Spot the escape route: talk to people who have left your profession recently.

- ☑ Distinguish dream from reality. If a new career or enterprise interests you, find out what you will be doing most of the time. The reality may not be as glamorous as you think. If you are head over heels in love with an idea, speak to at least one person who is thinking of getting out of that line of business. Find out why. Then match that with a balancing conversation with someone who loves their new career. Decide for yourself by matching what you hear to your own career drivers.

Finding a Careers Consultant

This chapter helps you to:

▌ Help yourself during career transition

▌ Understand the different kind of 'consultants' in the marketplace

▌ Identify who can provide help

▌ Know what to look for in a good careers consultant

Advice is what we ask for when we already know the answer but wish we didn't.

Erica Jong

HELPING YOURSELF

There are hundreds of careers books on the market. If they provided all the answers, no-one would be employed as a careers consultant. Reading a book like this one, you will probably hit one or two classic problems. The first is that you get 'stuck' somewhere. You've done the exercises, but you still can't see the wood for the trees. The second is that you need someone to see things that you can't see, and ask questions you can't ask yourself. Working with someone who can help you to brainstorm possibilities and suggest alternatives is important. And because career transition is as much about confidence as anything else, it's often vital to find people who will help you to see the best version of yourself, and help you to build up a positive picture of your skills, know-how and successes.

Apart from reading good books, listening to tapes and watching useful documentaries on career change and confidence building, another low-cost technique is to build yourself a **support group**. See Chapter 16 for more details.

However, there may come a time when you need the help of an experienced careers consultant. Here's how to find one.

CONSULTANTS, AND CONSULTANTS ...

There is a wide range of organizations which charge employers a fee for placing workers in jobs. They have different names, depending on the level of staff they place. At the lower end of the market you will find **employment** or **staffing agencies**. Agencies at this level tend to deal largely with temporary or contract work. Agencies working at higher levels tend to call themselves **recruitment** or **selection consultancies**, while those operating at the most senior end call themselves **selection** and/or **search** consultancies (also known as 'headhunters'). Chapter 11 gives you more detail about making the most of recruitment consultants.

In the UK recruitment consultancies, whatever their label, are not allowed to charge a fee to job seekers for finding them work. They can, however, charge a fee for a separate service such as producing a CV for you, but when they do this they should give you clear written terms of business when asking for your money.

Often a recruitment consultant can give you feedback on your CV, and on your overall 'message'. Again, take this advice with some caution and get a second opinion. Every recruiter has pet likes and dislikes when it comes to CVs, which usually relate to *the kind of candidates that they place most often*.

WHAT IS A CAREERS CONSULTANT?

People who can advise you on a career come in different guises. Here are a few of the categories of individuals and firms who work in the area of career guidance in the UK.

Career guidance for young people and those leaving the education system

Most people offering careers guidance work in the education sector. Types of support include:

- full-time or part-time **Careers Teachers** working in schools or colleges

- local **Careers Services**. These are mainly concerned with guidance and work placement for 16–18-year-olds, but do offer some advice for older career changers

- **Careers Advisers** working full-time in the higher education sector, largely working in **University Careers Services**. Advice and assistance are available to current students, graduates and, in some cases, older graduates who wish to undertake a career review.

Careers consultants or advisers dealing mainly with adults

Private sector careers consultancies are less common and more varied. Larger towns and cities usually have at least one. Most advisers working in this sector do not specifically have careers guidance qualifications. Some are experienced human resources, outplacement or recruitment specialists. Some are qualified occupational psychologists. Some will be qualified HR or careers specialists; most will have considerable business experience.

- **Outplacement** consultancies provide a service that is almost universally paid for by employers who are making staff redundant. Outplacement consultancies sometimes offer support to individuals paying for themselves, but the costs tend to be high.

▍ There are some larger **career consulting firms**, mainly in the major cities, whose charges approach those of outplacement firms. Such firms often offer a package of services, including CV writing and mailing out speculative letters.

▍ The former **Careers Service** has operations which compete with other private sector firms offering adult guidance.

▍ All of the above will be helpful if you want advice with your job search strategy, your CV or your interview technique. However, what you may be looking for is an experienced but relatively inexpensive **careers consultant/coach**. These individuals often work alone or in small organizations, and can help you to define where you want to go, and then help you to overcome the obstacles between you and your goals. Some consultants are gifted in helping you when you really don't know what kind of work you want. There are people in all of the above sectors who are good at this, but no one sector where you can guarantee getting this support.

For many, the best kind of support comes from individual careers consultants, or small firms who specialize in helping people with career transition.

HOW TO SPOT A CAREERS CONSULTANT

▍ It's always a good idea to ask around – word of mouth is often the best way. Ask people who have made a career change themselves.

▍ Your local Yellow Pages may take you straight to the right person, or try Yell.com to sweep a wider area.

▍ Some careers specialists are also qualified occupational psychologists.

▍ Be aware that many individual consultants are not exclusively career specialists. They may also work in coaching, training, personal development or recruitment. It's worth networking in all these fields to find the right person.

▮ Many personnel, recruitment or outplacement specialists are aware of someone in their region 'who does that sort of thing'.

CV writing services

A fairly large number of organizations specialize in writing CVs for you. They can be extremely helpful if you find it difficult to communicate your strengths in writing. The limitations on this service are that you can end up with a glossy, professional CV that is clearly not written by you, and sometimes that you don't get a CV that really communicates *your* message. It's generally best to write your own, and get help if you are stuck.

Warnings

There are firms of careers consultants out there who are prepared to take very large amounts of money off you. Sometimes they will provide an excellent service as a result. You can achieve similar results if you are able to find an individual consultant who charges on a different basis, and by supporting yourself.

A small number of firms will have access to exclusive databases. Some will actively market you. Be cautious when dealing with any firm that promises you access to hundreds of 'hidden' vacancies. This is the El Dorado of careers advice. What these firms are often offering is access to business networks, which is great, but no-one can guarantee you access to hidden vacancies, or tell you how many there are – by definition, they are hidden, not accessible in a predictable or measurable way. A professional careers consultant shouldn't take over the task for you, but give *you* the tools to develop and control your own career.

Charges

If your budget is very tight, see what is on offer from your local adult guidance provider or, if you are a graduate, the local

University Careers Service. You may be offered free assistance, or asked to pay a modest charge. The main limitations of such support are that you are not always advised by consultants with a great deal of business experience, and you may be offered only a relatively limited amount of time.

Private sector career consultancies' rates vary considerably. The larger the firm, the more likely it is that you will be sold a 'package' of meetings and support. You need to be sure from the outset that you need everything that is on offer, and that you feel confident that your money is going to be invested in the right kind of help, particularly if you need a lot of support working out what kind of work you want to do, and if you want to move into a completely new sector. A typical package fee ranges from £400 to £1000, but I have known fees as high as £15,000 to be quoted. You will sometimes have to pay VAT on top.

Careers consultants working on their own tend to have far lower overheads and lower fee levels. They may offer you a fee package, but will also often work on an hourly basis. Rates vary, in my experience, from £50 to £100 per hour outside London, and from £70 to £200 per hour in London. Cost, whether low or high, does not necessarily indicate value.

I think it's important for career changers to pay the right amount for advice. Too little, and the advice is not taken to heart because there is no sense of *investment in change*. Too much, and you add to your problem and debts.

Careers consultants are often experienced business profession-als who, in other spheres of commercial life, could be charging £1000 a day for their services. They won't – probably – be charging you on that basis. But you should expect to pay at least what you would pay on an hourly basis to a skilled professional such as an osteopath or a chiropractor.

What to ask

One approach is to ask about success rates, but you may find that any figures quoted on the time it takes to get a job, or the number of people assisted in the past, are not particularly helpful. In reality, everyone has a different set of needs. Some people just need a little job search coaching, while others need several months of exploring. The 'Must do' list at the end of this chapter provides a list of useful questions.

The really important thing is to talk to a consultant and work out whether he or she can help you. You may get a brief introductory session to discover this. Other consultants will wish to charge for this session, but don't let that put you off: an hour with an experienced consultant should provide you with a wide range of questions, ideas and insights, and so should be worth paying for.

'MUST DO' LIST: KEY QUESTIONS TO ASK A CAREERS CONSULTANT

- ☑ What is the hourly charge?

- ☑ Is there VAT on top?

- ☑ Am I committed to a programme of meetings? How much flexibility and choice do I have about the programme?

- ☑ How long does it normally take to the point where I have a fairly clear picture of what I have to offer, and where I want to be?

- ☑ Do you offer a free introductory session? If not, what information about your working style do you provide in advance? What kind of work are we likely to cover in a paid first session?

- ☑ Are you going to use any tests? If you are using ability, interest or psychometric tests are you qualified by the British Psychological Society to conduct these tests?

- ☑ Do you follow a Code of Practice?

- ☑ What happens if you feel you really can't help me? Or if *I* feel you can't help me?

☑   How do sessions work? Do you support clients by email or tele-
     phone?

☑   And, possibly the most important question: What strategies do
     you use to help people *who have no idea what they want to do
     next?*

Beginning it Here

This chapter introduces you to:

∎ ADEPT: your five-point action plan for getting a job you'll love

If you can fall in love with what you are going to do for a living, you've got it made.

George Burns

THE ADEPT MODEL

Much of this book has been dedicated to idea building, finding ways of coaching your brain to see new possibilities for your career. Reflection, imagining and planning all need to translate into activity.

Figure 16.1 takes you through all five stages of the ADEPT model, and shows how you can move from the reflection to action.

Far too many career changers attempt to use the kind of A–Z thinking demonstrated by Figure 13.1. We find ourselves with a career problem, and our normal response is immediately to begin a job search programme. The ADEPT model encourages you to invest in a few valuable hours of reflection and exploration before you swing into job search mode.

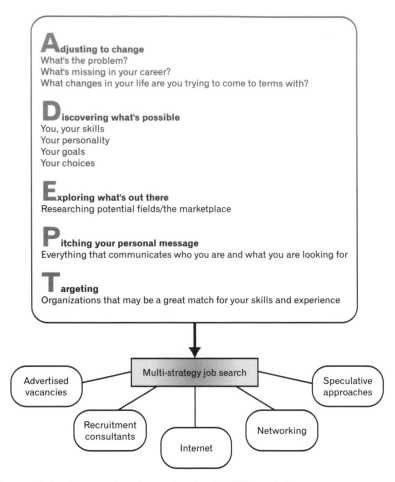

Figure 16.1 Career planning using the ADEPT model

The first step of the model, **A**djusting to change, is about your starting point: your mindset, constraints, and understanding what gets in the way of finding a job you'll love. Next you can move on to **D**iscovering what you have to offer by working through the exercises in this book. Before long you'll be itching to get to grips with something even more tangible, so the **E**xploring stage means finding out what's really out there.

Do this right, and you can move into multi-strategy job search (as outlined in Chapter 11). Ensure you include all the elements of the job search mix, particularly direct, speculative approaches to companies who are not advertising, and networking.

The next step of **P**itching your message is critical before you try to set yourself real **T**argets in terms of job search.

ACTIVITIES TO HELP YOU WORK THROUGH THE ADEPT MODEL

Get your message straight

Too many job changers try to win a job by pitching an unclear or untargeted message. Composing your message is, however, a key step in the ADEPT model. When it comes to job search, you are effectively a one-person marketing machine.

Composing a message is effectively writing a readily communicable wish list. Your message is contained in everything you send out (letters, CV, emails) and everything you say. It's what you say when someone asks you at a party 'what are you going to do next?'

When people are still licking their wounds from being treated badly by a past employer, feeling desperate enough to take anything, or they don't know what they are looking for, the negative experience becomes the biggest part of your message. It's easy for your CV and your interview performance to communicate a negative or uncertain message. You'll get sympathy, but you won't get past the first interview stage.

You will quickly learn that decision makers want to try to sum you up pretty quickly, and they are really only interested in their problems, not yours. Therefore it helps to prepare strong presentation statements (see Chapter 7). It's also vitally important to both job search and networking that you have a short, coherent message that sums up what you are about.

Your One-Sentence Message

As a careers coach I encourage all my clients to compose a short message – a message that you can get across almost in one breath. Something that sums up who you are and where you want to get to. The sentence sounds something like this:

> Your One-Sentence Message
>
> *'I want to do a job that allows me to do A and B and C in an organization that's doing X and Y and Z.'*

The A and B and C are your motivated skills – the things you do best. X, Y and Z describe the key ingredients in the mix as far as your next employer is concerned. You might be talking about what the organization actually produces or the services it provides. You might also talk about the style (high-tech, customer-focused …) and culture of the organization (private, public, blue chip, privately owned …).

Employers, recruitment consultants and networking contacts respond well to this kind of message because it is clear, succinct, memorable and packed with enthusiasm. What's more, people respond in a completely different way compared to simply asking about job opportunities. When they hear your message, listeners hear a set of ingredients that hasn't yet formed into a recipe. They say things like 'You know, you really should talk to my friend Rashid …' or 'Have you thought about talking to Acme Industries …' or, best of all, 'That sounds to me like …' – when they identify a sector or field you haven't yet fallen across.

This kind of message is also great for interviews (especially when you meet the question 'tell me about yourself' or 'why do you want this job?', and very handy when someone at a barbecue or party says 'what would you like to do, ideally?'

Recruit a support team

Few things are achievable without the right tools and the right people, yet all too many people try to break out of their career box alone. Get support. First of all, have experimental, 'what if?' conversations with as many people you can who can give you a different perspective (but make sure the feedback is at least objective, and preferably upbeat). Secondly – and do this before you finish this book – build a support team.

You may also find it helpful to have some input from a career consultant. See Chapter 15 for ways of finding someone who can help.

Support trios

Find **two** other people who will help. They don't need to be in the same situation as you, but they do need to be curious about people, jobs and the world. One other person will do, at a push, but a coach/pupil relationship often happens when there are only two people. With a trio meeting together regularly you get two perspectives on everything that's said. The conversation doesn't need to be just about you – you can help each other in turn. You'll often find that a trio discussion over a bottle of wine works very nicely.

Recruit the two members of your trio carefully. They should be people who can:

▌ support you in the ups and downs of career transition

▌ give you honest, objective advice about your skills, and help you to see the evidence you use to back them up

▌ give you ideas for exploration and connections with other people who can help

▌ use 'yellow hat' thinking (see Table 8.3) to support your ideas. If you say 'I'm thinking of becoming an astronaut', they will be the sort of people who will say 'How would that work for you? What would be the spin-offs? What first step could you take? How can you get to speak to someone who's been into space ... ?'

Warning: if you hear a friend say 'Yes, but, in the real world ...' or 'It's not that simple ...' or even 'That won't work', don't invite them to be part of this process. There are thousands of people out there who will be all too happy to pour cold water on your ideas. Career success is as much about motivation as it is about strategy. Choose people who will give you positive, encouraging messages.

I use the example of someone who has been into space as a genuine example. In my life I have been within half a mile of two famous astronauts (Yuri Gagarin, when I was in my pram and he was guest of honour in Manchester, and Neil Armstrong when he spoke in Tatton Park in Cheshire some 40 years later). I regularly ask large audiences 'Who's met someone who has been into space?' The first time I asked, a woman in the second row put her hand up, and told me afterwards that it was one of the most amazing discussions of her life. You could probably fit everyone who has been into space into a small coach, but in the average audience one person in 80 or so has talked to someone who has been there. Even the most extraordinary people are not that far away.

Record and build

As you come to the end of this book, you will have discovered a great deal of information. It may be hard at this stage to see the wood for the trees. Table 16.1 gives you an example of one method of combining information. Ideally this should be on a single sheet of paper. Write down the key ingredients, and then let the idea mull. Stick the sheet on a fridge or wardrobe door. Let your unconscious brain make connections for you. Show it to friends, colleagues, your support group. This sheet is a great way of focusing on your strengths and building ideas for your future.

Table 16.1   Master sheet

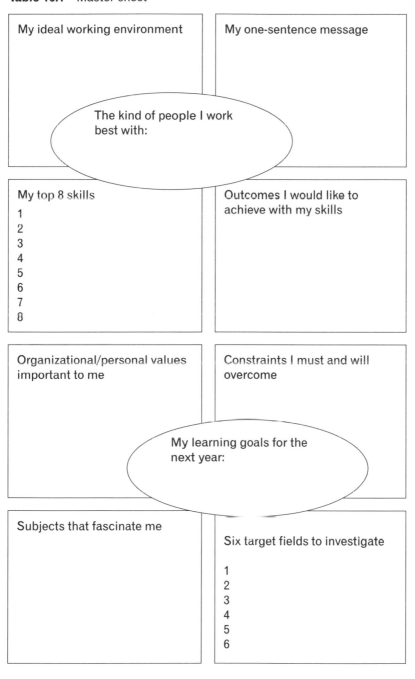

My ideal working environment	My one-sentence message

The kind of people I work best with:

My top 8 skills	Outcomes I would like to
1	achieve with my skills
2	
3	
4	
5	
6	
7	
8	

Organizational/personal values important to me	Constraints I must and will overcome

My learning goals for the next year:

Subjects that fascinate me	Six target fields to investigate
	1
	2
	3
	4
	5
	6

Job: what you do to support your vocation.

Anonymous

Pass it on

Once you've found what you're looking for, give it away.

Once you have learned some of the solutions to your own career problems, what will you do with that information? With luck and a little application you'll move towards a job you love doing. When you discover anything, you can hold it to yourself, or you can pass it on.

The only true reason for career breakthrough is that we become equipped to improve the working lives of those around us. That may sound madly altruistic, but skills discovery is hollow if it's only about *me*. First of all we discover our talents – the solo instrument we play. The exploration continues until we hear the other instruments as well and understand our role in the orchestra. The final step is to help others to begin to hear the music.

Key Checklists

Exploration is rather hollow if it doesn't take you anywhere. This chapter provides a wide range of activity tools for getting the job you'll love.

A – What kind of career is right for you?

B – Designing a winning CV

C – What to put on the first page of your CV

D – What to put in your CV

E – What NOT to do with your CV

F – The essentials of a great covering letter

G – Preparing for an interview

H – Tough interview questions to prepare for (and what to say)

I – Questions to ask prospective employers

J – Advice for older jobseekers

K – Online job search and job applications

A – WHAT KIND OF CAREER IS RIGHT FOR YOU?

1. Do you want to work *mainly* with **things**, **people**, **information** or **concepts**?

2. Think about your **career drivers** – do you want to catalogue the world, change the world, help the world, sell the world ...?

3. How much **independence** do you want to have about the way you work and make decisions? If you find it difficult to take instructions or you want to go your own way, maybe self-employment beckons.

4. Look for organizations that reflect your feelings about **rules**. Are you happier working within a clear set of guidelines, or in a completely open-ended way?

5. What activities, products or ideas seem **meaningful** to you? You don't need to be inspired by biscuit technology or soap powder, but if you find any serious discussion about them just absurd, keep looking.

6. What kind of work have you **chosen** to do, either in your leisure time or as a volunteer? Often the work we *choose* to do without financial constraint is a great clue to our best work.

7. What kind of companies or products reflect your **personal beliefs** about life, other people, spirituality, the planet, etc.?

8. Look at the **skills** you *really* enjoy using, when you are impossible to distract and rarely bored. Where could you use them?

9. What subjects *really* **interest** you? How can you translate your interests into fields of work?

10. Ask. **Find out**. Don't use your career as a lab experiment. Talk to people about the jobs they do. Learn from the mistakes others have made. Get careers advice.

B – DESIGNING A WINNING CV

1. There are many different ways of setting out a CV. The most important thing to remember is that your CV will be read, on average, in under 20 seconds.

2. This means that the first page of your CV does most of the work. See Checklist C for more details about the content of the first page.

3. The example CV on pages 250–1 gives you an idea for setting the first page of your CV out in blocks of information. In this case the blocks are as follows:

■ your contact details

■ a profile which summarizes who you are and what you're looking for

■ your key achievements and experience

■ your most important professional and academic qualifications

■ a quick summary of your career to date.

C – WHAT TO PUT ON THE FIRST PAGE OF YOUR CV

1. Remember your CV will be screened into a 'yes' or 'no' pile. Do everything you can on page 1 to end up in the 'yes' pile.

2. A reader will probably have made a decision about you before getting to the end of your first page. Make sure any **key information** is here.

3. Think of the first page of your CV as a **one-page advertisement**, which should be strong enough to stand alone.

4. Don't put anything on the front page that strikes a negative note, such as difficulties you had with a past employer, or a failed course.

5. Include your contact details at the top of page 1. Include an email address, and make sure it is businesslike. 'Happy-golucky@freebie.com' conveys the wrong impression.

6. Use summary words such as 'qualified' or 'graduate' to get your message across in the profile.

7. Don't include **empty adjectives**. Almost everyone is creative, dynamic, enthusiastic …. Focus on what you can do well.

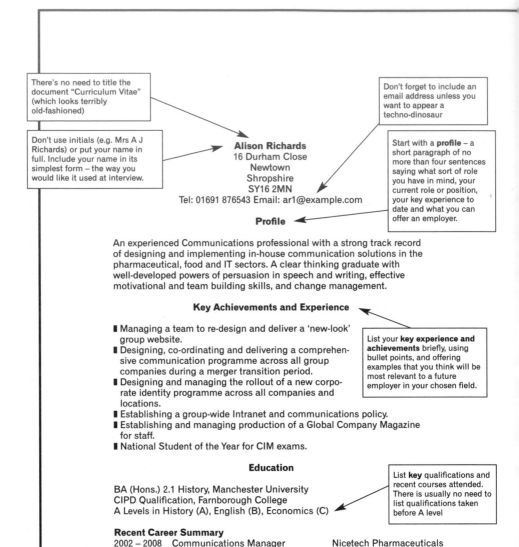

There's no need to title the document "Curriculum Vitae" (which looks terribly old-fashioned)

Don't use initials (e.g. Mrs A J Richards) or put your name in full. Include your name in its simplest form – the way you would like it used at interview.

Don't forget to include an email address unless you want to appear a techno-dinosaur

Alison Richards
16 Durham Close
Newtown
Shropshire
SY16 2MN
Tel: 01691 876543 Email: ar1@example.com

Profile

Start with a **profile** – a short paragraph of no more than four sentences saying what sort of role you have in mind, your current role or position, your key experience to date and what you can offer an employer.

An experienced Communications professional with a strong track record of designing and implementing in-house communication solutions in the pharmaceutical, food and IT sectors. A clear thinking graduate with well-developed powers of persuasion in speech and writing, effective motivational and team building skills, and change management.

Key Achievements and Experience

▌ Managing a team to re-design and deliver a 'new-look' group website.
▌ Designing, co-ordinating and delivering a comprehensive communication programme across all group companies during a merger transition period.
▌ Designing and managing the rollout of a new corporate identity programme across all companies and locations.
▌ Establishing a group-wide Intranet and communications policy.
▌ Establishing and managing production of a Global Company Magazine for staff.
▌ National Student of the Year for CIM exams.

List your **key experience and achievements** briefly, using bullet points, and offering examples that you think will be most relevant to a future employer in your chosen field.

Education

BA (Hons.) 2.1 History, Manchester University
CIPD Qualification, Farnborough College
A Levels in History (A), English (B), Economics (C)

List **key** qualifications and recent courses attended. There is usually no need to list qualifications taken before A level

Recent Career Summary
2002 – 2008	Communications Manager	Nicetech Pharmaceuticals
1999 – 2002	Internal Communications Manager	Chocolate UK
1992 – 1999	HR and Communications Manager	Giant Telcoms
1986 – 1992	HR Assistant	Giant Telcoms

Your career ladder – at a glance

From page 2 onwards, discuss each job you have done (most recent job first). Summarize the job in 2–3 lines, then set out your key achievements in bullet points

Detailed Career Summary

COMMUNICATIONS MANAGER, NICETECH   **2001 TO DATE**

Use active language such as 'initiated', 'organised', 'managed', 'led'.

Responsible for setting and rolling out policy regarding internal communications, and for managing an in-house communication team.
- Designed, co-ordinated and delivered a comprehensive internal communication programme across all European locations, with particular emphasis within the UK.
- Introduced a European Newsletter – sourced business, technical and human-interest stories from 9 European sites, organized translation services.
- Initiated, designed and implemented a new group-wide company Intranet.

INTERNAL COMMUNICATIONS MANAGER – CHOCOLATE UK (1998-2001)

Responsible for all aspects of internal communications, and for launching and editing an in-house magazine.
- Initiated a communications programme reaching out to 13,500 staff across Europe.
- Organized and managed a very successful Royal Visit to open our new site.
- Produced a 'diary-style' video of the preparations for, and the actual Royal Visit.
- Organized groundbreaking ceremony and Public Relations activities for a multi-company training initiative.
- Member of the Site Executive Management Team responsible for managing an HR team, providing a comprehensive generalist HR service supporting 300 people.
- Introduced our site-wide Team Briefing process – ran training sessions for managers.

Include facts, numbers and percentages where possible

HR & COMMS MANAGER, GIANT TELECOMS (1992-1998)
Initially an HR role, this was expanded in 1996 to include a responsibility for all HR activities including: communications, recruitment, remuneration, 'downsizing', employee relations, performance management, training and development.
- Launched a management development programme leading to Investors in People (IIP) status.
- Researched, designed and implemented a 'shop floor to top floor' pay and grading system.
- Designed and introduced a competency-based appraisal and recruitment programme.

Explain jargon or abbreviations if this helps the reader

List significant awards or targets achieved

CONTINUING PROFESSIONAL DEVELOPMENT
Web page design using FrontPage (2001)
SHL Ability Testing and Personality Profiling (1999)
Handling the Media (1997)
Facilitator Training (1997)
Presentation Skills (1996)
Management Skills Programme
I am a regular user of the following software packages: Microsoft Word, PowerPoint, Excel, Outlook, Project, FrontPage 2000, Photoshop CS

List additional qualifications achieved, learning, and training courses attended. Refer to your skill level with IT packages

INTERESTS
Hill walking, Trustee of local disability charity, travelling and learning to improve my spoken Italian.

Include interests that might be relevant to the job, those that indicate co-operative or team working, or simply things you can talk about at interview with enthusiasm

8. Include any **key qualifications** on page 1 if you know this is an important benchmark for an employer.

9. Match your key achievements and experience to the top 5 or 6 items required by the job.

10. Include a career history in brief so the reader gets a complete overview of your career history to date (give a detailed account of each job on page 2, starting with your most recent job).

D – WHAT TO PUT IN YOUR CV (see example CV)

1. Remember – a CV only has one function: to get you an interview.

2. Make your CV immediately interesting.

3. Keep it **concise**. It isn't your life story.

4. Your CV should make **claims** about who you are and what you can do, and then provide evidence to back up those claims.

5. **Translate** what you know and can do into terms that will appeal to a recruiter – talk about solving problems, making a difference, etc.

6. Try to say something interesting about your **academic history** – relate it to an employer's needs rather than regurgitating the syllabus, e.g. if you led a seminar or gave a talk, write about your facilitation or presentation skills.

7. It's all very well being the best thing since sliced bread. **Be specific**: try to express **achievements** in terms of awards, money, time or percentages.

8. Use good-quality white paper.

9. Include something under 'interests' that is neither bland nor run of the mill. Include interests that make you appear a rounded person, and those that have some relevance to the job. Make sure you can talk enthusiastically for at least 5 minutes on any interest you mention.

10. Take some time to make the layout attractive, with plenty of white space. Don't print text so small it's painful to read.

E – WHAT NOT TO DO WITH YOUR CV

1. **Don't** put any information on page 1 unless it says something important about you that might get you an interview.

2. **Don't** provide huge amounts of detail about jobs you did more than 10 years ago.

3. **Don't** put yourself down, or try irony or humour. It rarely reads the way you want it to.

4. **Don't** give the names and addresses of referees – you can provide them if they are requested, but you should brief your referees carefully about who they may be talking to, and what the potential job is all about.

5. **Don't** use obscure abbreviations or jargon.

6. **Don't** include your age or the dates you qualified.

7. **Don't** disclose your salary unless you think this is going to be specifically helpful to an employer – it's generally best to deal with this at interview or, if you have to, in a covering letter.

8. **Don't** include non-essential personal information, e.g. height, weight, names of your children, or your religious or political beliefs.

9. **Don't** send out poor photocopies. Ideally, print your CV out on good-quality paper each time.

10. **Don't** include your reasons for leaving jobs, but be prepared to discuss this at interview in a positive way.

F – THE ESSENTIALS OF A GREAT COVERING LETTER

1. The only function of this letter is to get your CV read, and to get you a meeting. Think of your letter like the first page of your CV, as a one-page **advertisement** for you. Make your letter **brief, enthusiastic and interesting**.

2. Ensure that **everything** in the reader's name, job title and address is correct.

3. Try not to begin every sentence and paragraph with 'I'. Focus on the **reader** of the letter and his or her perspective.

4. **Research** – refer to the problems, opportunities and headaches that your target company is facing.

5. Indicate in brief paragraphs **what** you are applying for, **who** you are, **why** you are interested, and **what** you have to offer. Don't oversell. State briefly why you are a good **match** for the job.

6. Refer the reader to your enclosed CV. Pick three or four of your top **achievements** and repeat them in the letter, using different terms to the way you have expressed them in your CV. Choose achievements relevant to the job.

7. Don't put anything in your covering letter that gives the reader an excuse to put the letter aside, e.g. apologizing for your lack of a particular requirement, or mentioning your age, or referring to negative aspects such as why you left your last job.

8. If your letter is a **speculative** approach (i.e. to a company that isn't currently advertising a job), try to ensure that your letter is read by a **named decision maker**.

9. Think carefully what **action** you are asking for. If you are seeking a meeting, ask for one.

10. **Telephone to check** that your letter has been received by the intended recipient. Ask one relevant question, or mention one reason why you might be able to help the employer, and suggest a meeting.

G – PREPARING FOR AN INTERVIEW

1. **Plan** carefully. Do you know where you are going and how to get there? Who are you seeing?

2. Make sure you know the **names** of the people who will be interviewing you. Practise saying them if they are difficult to pronounce.

3. There's no such thing as enough **preparation** for an interview. Find out everything you can about the company and what it makes or does. Look for current news – show you are up to date.

4. Why does this job exist? What problems will it solve? What are the **key result areas**?

5. Remember: **employers buy experience**. Think about what **evidence of achievement** you can talk about in the interview; rehearse your success stories.

6. Work out what is **appropriate** in terms of everything you present, including yourself. Look the part, and you will feel it. Dress as if you are already doing the job.

7. Second guess the **employer's 'shopping list'** from the job details. What skills, qualities and experience do you have to match?

8. Be your own worst interview nightmare. What is the most **difficult question** you might have to face? Practise the answer. Practise again.

9. **Be upbeat**. Employers latch on to negative messages, so don't give them any.

10. **Prepare for rejection**. On balance you will be rejected more times than accepted. Even if you don't get the job, you can learn a huge amount about your perceived market value. Remember, there's a job out there for you somewhere – more people are working in the UK than ever before.

H – TOUGH INTERVIEW QUESTIONS TO PREPARE FOR (AND WHAT TO SAY)

1. **'Tell us about yourself.'** Prepare for the worst – a classic opener that can really throw you. Have a *brief* summary statement up your sleeve.

2. **'Where do you see yourself in 5 years' time?'** If your answer doesn't ring true for you, it won't for anyone else. Talk about career plans, and what you want to learn and achieve in the future.

3. **'Why do you want this job?'** Have a clear answer to this (even if, privately, you're not sure – you only have to decide when the job offer is in your hand).

4. **'What kind of person are you?'** Handle questions about personality carefully. Rather than say 'I'm an ideas person', talk about a time when you changed things with a good idea.

5. **'Why did you leave … ?'** Employers will probe for reasons for job change. If you are currently out of work, they will probe this, too. Rehearse short, simple, positive 'stories' to cover these points. This is *not* telling lies, just a simple, positive summary. (See Chapter 7 on presentation statements.)

6. **'How will you cope in a crisis?'** Have a couple of good examples of past triumphs up your sleeve.

7. **'How will you …'** questions are beginning to create a **future** which includes *you* – so welcome them. Describe what you would do within the organization as if you are there already. Create the right picture, and the employer won't be able to imagine life without you.

8. **'Why are you looking for a job right now?'** Rehearse a brief, upbeat answer that covers redundancy or unemployment. Don't bleat on about how difficult the market is, or how many rejections you're received.

9. **'What do you need to earn?'** Wrong question. Focus on the value you can add to the employer, not your basic needs. Find out what the company is willing to pay, or work out what similar employers pay for good people.

10. **'What are your weaknesses?'** Remember that the recruiter gives far more weight to negative information. Switch the subject to your strengths as soon as possible.

I – QUESTIONS TO ASK PROSPECTIVE EMPLOYERS

1. **Read between the lines** – what does the job description fail to tell you?

2. Make sure you communicate real **interest**, e.g. 'What are the company's biggest problems/headaches/opportunities?'

3. 'Where does the company plan to be in 12 months?' Try to work out what time with the company will do for your CV.

4. Try to find out how you will be **measured** once you begin the job – are there any set targets? Is there a formal appraisal system?

5. What **learning opportunities** (courses, qualifications, training) does the job offer?

6. What **variety** is there in the job?

7 What kind of **support** will you get? Is there a formal mentoring or coaching programme?

8. Find out what you can about **standards** and **expectations**. How will you know if you have been successful?

9. Watch out for **buying signals** – usually when the conversation switches from past to future. Wait until they want you – that's a good time to negotiate your salary.

10. If you feel you have a chance, **ask for the job**. It might just work.

J – ADVICE FOR OLDER JOBSEEKERS

1. Don't draw attention to your age by giving emphasis to the year you started work, or by highlighting out of date terminology, organization names or qualifications.

2. For the same reason, it's generally not a good idea to refer to the ages of your adult **children** (they may be older than the person interviewing you!).

3. Finally, it may not be useful to indicate the year you obtained your **qualifications**. It may seem like ancient history to the recruiter.

4. Make your CV focus on **what you have achieved** and **what you have to offer**, not on your age.

5. Include an **email address**. Employers often assume that older workers are not IT literate.

6. Remember that employers buy experience. Demonstrate how your **know-how and maturity** will be a benefit.

7. Don't focus on the bad news stories. Look at the high proportion of men and women in your age group who do find work, and build on their **success strategies**.

8. Try not to reminisce ('in my day …'). **Talk about the future**. Show flexibility and a willingness to learn.

9. Explore the possibilities of a **portfolio career** (see Chapter 14).

10. **Don't** apologize for your age or lack of recent relevant experience, and do not convey desperation.

K – ONLINE JOB SEARCH AND JOB APPLICATIONS

1. **Be proactive**. Every month new employers switch to online recruiting, so don't leave online applications out of the mix. But don't use online job search instead of other methods, or as an excuse for not speaking to real people.

2. Remember the range of **resources** online: vacancy listings, CV databases, Internet-based career centres, self-assessment tools useful in career search, search engines to help you to find companies and organizations, trade associations and professional bodies, as well as news and information services.

3. **Check sites regularly** and learn how to use the relevant search criteria.

4. Don't define your search too early, too soon. Use **broad categories** at first, then use search tools to refine the listings.

5. Electronic job applications, like conventional applications, need a **brief covering letter**. Format this as neatly as a printed letter, and cover the essentials: what the job is, why you are applying for it, what you have to offer.

6. Compose a CV in **plain text** ('Text Only') form in a word-processing package. Ignore all text effects except for capital letters. Do not use tabs or columns. Once you have a clear layout you can then copy and paste your CV onto a jobsite.

7. Make your electronic CV concise: be exact, be interesting and communicate your strengths. Do not clutter your online CV with unnecessary detail – think about someone searching for **key words** rather than a whole CV.

8. Give your CV a **title**, and make it work for you – don't just use a job title or a field, but something clear, e.g. 'Senior Human Resources/Training Manager'.

9. Set up **more than one CV** – think about the different kinds of employer that may be hunting for you online.

10. **Renew your CV** every month or so. If you do this, the database will usually treat your document as a new CV and put it to the top of the electronic pile.

Informational Interviews: The REVEAL Method

The REVEAL method is a form of informational interviewing, a method for finding out more about a field of work. To do this you are going to identify key individuals who will love to talk about their industry sector. You will add to your personal knowledge, increase your network and learn how jobs 'feel' from the inside.

The principle is *research before job search*. You are not making a once-and-for-all career decision or trying to get a subversive job interview. You are simply finding out vital pieces of information to move your career transition forward:

■ What kinds of roles exist?

■ What organizations are out there?

■ Would I find the job interesting?

■ How do people get into this field or occupation?

Informational interviews are most definitely not about job search, at least not directly. Think about the way you would react if someone contacted you at work and asked to see you. If the caller said 'I'd appreciate your help in identifying jobs in your organization', you'd feel pretty uncomfortable. You don't know the caller, so why should you recommend this person for a post? *Think about what your contact can actually deliver*. Most people are happy talking about themselves and the job they do, and usually happy to give you information and contacts if the meeting goes well. Don't even ask questions that are partly about job search ('I'd like your advice on my CV' or 'I'd appreciate an early tip-off if any jobs are advertised'). If the interview goes well, this will probably be offered anyway.

WHAT DO *REVEAL* INTERVIEWS ACHIEVE?

■ You get to put smart business clothes on and see people in their place of work, which boosts your confidence.

■ You get to meet real people in real jobs. Your understanding about career routes, job roles and employers moves from desk research to field research. You learn about entry routes to careers, about organizational structures and cultures, and you get a real 'feel' for a large number of employers.

■ You get to spend time inside organizations, which gives you a huge amount of material to draw upon at interview.

■ People remember you, and make connections on your behalf.

■ You are often talking to decision makers, so you get some real insights about the evidence to use in an actual job interview.

■ It's a process that helps you to decide which career path to take, because you've seen a job from the inside.

■ If you're tracking down people who are passionate about a field of work that calls you strongly, you will probably end up with some very interesting new contacts and friends.

■ You fall over jobs. It's true. You fall over jobs in the hidden job market. Ironically, the indirect route which is not focused on job search often turns out to be the number one strategy for getting at the hidden job market.

HOW TO GET MEETINGS

Think of the toughest way of doing it. It's possible to work your way through the Yellow Pages or to turn up at the reception and demand a meeting, but it's an uphill struggle. If you approach an organization as a stranger, the first question in the contact's mind is 'what am I being sold?' (followed swiftly by 'is this someone asking for a job?'). If you think of informational interviews as hard-nosed networking, you've found the perfect excuse not to do them.

Always begin with people you know

This is the vital step. Do this right and you never have to make a terrifying phone call. Begin with three people who you can approach without any hesitation. Practise on friends and colleagues if you need to build confidence. These three people may simply be asked the question 'who do you know in the field of X … ?'

Begin by asking yourself 'What questions do I need answering?' These will be questions about fields of work, about industry sectors, about entry routes, about potential growth areas. Can't think of anyone? Use the technique outlined in Exercise 11.1. Don't miss out your family. Often we never ask those near and dear to us who it is they know. Even people who never think about networking usually have about 100 people within their immediate contact circle. Starting with friends, neighbours and family, conduct REVEAL interviews or ask 'who do you know?' until you get to the point where you have **three initial contacts** who can begin to answer your main career questions.

At this stage, the main purpose is to gain the names and contact details of people you can approach. However, knowing a name is not enough. You're back in the uncomfortable situation of cold calling. So what you do, in every case, is to say to your contact something like this: 'I hate ringing people cold. Would you be kind enough to telephone ahead for me, just to say who I am and what the conversation will be about?' Always ask people to ring ahead, and that way you should never be beginning a conversation 'You don't know me, but …'.

If every interview really is about information, and you are brief and businesslike in the way you conduct the meeting, there is no reason at all why your contact won't be happy to make a call on your behalf. That way your next contact will (usually) take your call and will have a sense what your conversation will be about, trusting that you aren't going to ask them to do something too demanding.

When you speak to your next contact (by telephone):

1. Mention your name and the person who recommended you to call. This should be a good enough memory prompt ('Oh, yes – Bill called me about you'). Look for personal connections between one contact and the next ('Bill tells me you're a keen fell walker ...').

2. Give a brief reminder about why you want a discussion. If necessary, make it clear that you are *not* selling anything, *not* undertaking market research and *not* asking for a job interview.

3. Ask for a face-to-face meeting. Say that you'd like to ask a short number of key questions. Ask for *11 minutes* of the person's time. '5 minutes' or '15 minutes' is too vague.

4. Contacts will often try to get you to have the conversation on the phone. Be honest: say that you learn much more by visiting people in their own organizations. If you can't get past a phone interview, try to get a link to someone else you can see face-to-face.

CONDUCTING A REVEAL INTERVIEW

When you get to the meeting

When you get a face-to-face meeting, you're ready to use the REVEAL method, as set out in Table A.1. The first few times you use the method it's probably wise to stick to this structure (although find a way of wording the questions which works for you; don't use the script parrot-fashion). Later on you can develop your own questions.

Table A.1   The REVEAL method of informational interviewing

Stages of REVEAL	Notes
Recap	**Key statement:**
	'I am here because …'
	Remind the listener of who introduced you, why you want the meeting and what you want to get out of it. It always helps to say that you have been recommended to speak to your contact.
	Make it clear that you will be asking for referrals at the end of the conversation. You might say at the outset that your plan is to talk to a dozen people who really know what's going on in a particular sector. At the end of the interview you can then happily ask for further contacts.
Explore	**Key statement and question:**
	'I'm here to find out as much as I can about …. What do you find most interesting/challenging about working in this sector?'
	This is your chance to ask key questions about the industry or sector being explored.
Vision	**Key questions:**
	'What changes can you see in this sector in the next 2 years? What kind of person will do well in this changing sector?'
	This should give you some useful data on anticipated changes, and the ideal skills profile of successful candidates. It may also flag up magazines you should be reading, and exhibitions and conferences you should be attending.

Entry routes	**Key question:**
	'How do people normally get into this line of work?'
	Probe the conventional *and* unconventional ways of getting work in this sector. There are usually non-standard routes into most careers.

Action	**Key question:**
	'What should I do to find out more?'
	Make sure your interview ends with concrete results: ideas for new connections, other organizations, sources of research.

Links	**Key statement and questions:**
	'Thanks very much for your time today. As I mentioned before, I'm keen to talk to a number of people in this field. Who else should I be talking to?' Can you please recommend two or three other people who can give me an equally useful perspective?
	This is an issue you have flagged up earlier in the process. Show how appreciative you are, otherwise your request sounds a little like 'is there anyone I can talk to more useful than you?'
	If no names are forthcoming, probe for:
	1. Names of organizations
	2. Names of network conveners, e.g. branch Chairs ot trade associations
	3. (If nothing else is forthcoming) the names of good recruitment consultants dealing with this field.
	And finally, ALWAYS ask your contact to phone ahead to the next round of contacts, so once again you can avoid having to begin a conversation 'you don't know me, but … '.

What if I am invited to consider a job?

Don't let the meeting become a job interview – that's a breach of trust. If a specific position enters the discussion, say you'd like to go away and prepare for a proper interview. Offer a time when you are free within the next few days. Ask for full details of the job and prepare thoroughly, even if you are in a shortlist of one. That way you come back fully prepared, matching your selling points to the key requirements of the job.

Building on each interview

From your three initial contacts you can easily get to speak to 30–40 people in 2–3 months. For some people these conversations are the start of lifelong friendships.

First of all, decide what record-keeping system you are going to use so that you can build up a personal web methodically. You'll need to retain telephone and fax numbers as well as addresses, both real and email. You'll also need to be able to cross-link records, and keep a note of the areas you discuss, and a diary reminder of any action or follow-up you have agreed.

'MUST DO' LIST: GROUND RULES OF THE REVEAL METHOD

- ☑ Use the structure. Be confident.
- ☑ Don't exceed the time limit unless it is at the other person's insistence.
- ☑ Don't ask to be shown round the building or site, but warmly accept the offer if it is made.
- ☑ Don't offer your CV or ask about specific job openings (but have a CV to hand in case it is asked for).

☑ Be prepared for the question 'and what about you?' This is a good chance to try out your key message (see Chapter 15).

☑ Don't neglect the critical final step of asking for three other contacts. It's very easy to walk out of a meeting missing one of the main reasons for the interview.

☑ If the conversation isn't generating contact names of individuals, remember you can ask for (a) names of organizations or (b) names of good recruitment consultants in this sector.

☑ Keep a record of each interview, who you have seen and all connections made.

☑ Send a thank you card afterwards: it's an unexpected gesture, and you will be remembered. Recipients are often touched by the gesture and keep your card for a long time. Put your name, email address and telephone number somewhere discreetly on the card.

☑ Remember that some people will turn down your request for a meeting. Think carefully about whether this is the result of what you have done, or simply because the contact was too busy or indifferent to give you a meeting. Approached the right way through an intermediate contact, about four out of five requests lead to informational interviews.

☑ If all else fails at any stage, fall back on your last ditch question: 'who else should I be talking to?'

People Who Have Transformed Their Careers

The article below appeared in *Coaching at Work* (May/June 2008) (see www.cipd.co.uk/coachingatwork for full details of the magazine).

The article, featuring John's work and case studies, is primarily of interest to career coaches, but also contains information which readers may find useful about what gets in the way in career change. The case studies are from clients who built their career change around ideas contained in this book.

ADVICE FOR THE RUDDERLESS

Dealing with the major obstacles in career coaching

Career coaching is about helping clients to explore the difference between comforting fantasies and goals. Working fantasies are important – imagining yourself on a desert island may be a healthy antidote to the drudgery of work. However, these are pipe-dreams that we have no intention of acting upon, while goals require activity, first steps.

For me, the heart of career coaching is the question *'how is this decision going to be made?'*. If the question is, as it is for many, *'what do I feel called to do?'*, the routine straight-line thinking we do in business life rarely works. Exciting career change

WILL BEALE, 37, HEAD OF PROGRAMME MANAGEMENT, WWF-UK

Will studied Natural Sciences and Chemical Engineering before joining Unilever. He worked in research, manufacturing, and new product development, but after ten years had a strong impulse to find his ideal career path.

Will began feeling apprehensive, but threw himself positively into the process: *'I spent three months undertaking informational interviews with about 40 people in my target fields. I learned a lot but it was also quite a tough time, especially for my family.'*

Will applied for a wide range of jobs – business, NGOs, public sector. Will comments: *'John sometimes advised me not to apply for jobs because they would not move me forward.'*

His dream was to work for an organization actively contributing to animal protection. When a job at the World Wildlife Fund entered his sights he felt he had found the perfect match: *'It seemed ideal but honestly I did not expect to get it. However by this time my application, interview and negotiation skills were well practised, and I knew how to sell the positive about myself.'*

At WWF Will has moved from quality management to building excellence in conservation management. Will continues to enjoy his work enormously, and recognises that the change he has made is part of deeper life choices – *'it's an analytical role but requires a lot of people skills. I have travelled widely (whilst endeavouring to minimize flights) and have a much broader perspective on the world. Through the whole process of change, my personal faith and my prayer life were very important in sustaining me towards finding my mission in life.'*

SIMON BARBER, CHIEF EXECUTIVE, 5 BOROUGHS PARTNERSHIP NHS TRUST

Chartered Accountant Simon Barber left United Utilities and a long career in the commercial world, after undertaking a senior role in Your Communications.

Simon found John Lees through the services of Career Management Consultants Ltd: *'I felt that my skills and experience could be useful to the public sector, ideally in the NHS, and that this would be more personally rewarding. John advised me to take my time and really use the opportunity to examine where I wanted to go next, to identify what I enjoyed doing and what really drives me. I think John thought it was a tall order to move role and sector, but he never wavered in his support.'*

A clear strategy developed: *'I learned the power of developing a network – of simply picking up the phone or sending a short letter to ask how I might help in my target sector. This took me outside my comfort zone – I had been very confident in the internal network of UU but I was very reluctant to approach people I didn't know.'*

Simon learned a great deal from new contacts inside the sector, who pointed to the value of short term assignments. The turning point came when Simon received a 'no' letter on a permanent job at Christie's Hospital, then turned it into a conversation about the organization's needs and into a breakthrough short-term assignment.

For Simon *'that moved the conversation from the theoretical to the specific.'* Simon focused on the way health authorities were required to make radical changes by the Department of Health, and became appointed as the Turnaround Director for a high profile PCT where he reduced a deficit of £42.6m by just under £14m in 12 months.

Having started with recruiters telling him that a move into the health sector was all uphill, Simon became Chief Executive of 5 Boroughs Partnership Trust (a specialist mental health trust covering Warrington, St Helens, Knowsley, Wigan and Halton), beating 50 other applicants to the job, many of whom had far more health sector experience.

involves taking at least one risky step, which is usually asking the question 'what if … ?' That requires divergent, right-brain thinking, and often a dumping of conventional wisdom about what's out there, and what kind of people enjoy exciting careers.

Decision-making is in fact a form of controlled discovery, and that only works where career changers are prepared to step to the edge of their comfort zone, and sometimes beyond. All three case studies here did exactly that – rejecting initial advice from recruitment consultants about what was the realistic, no-brainer next step, they all pursued active enquiries with actual post-holders, often exploring several fields of work at the same time.

It's all about moving into active mode, taking control. In passive mode many of us can't seem to find the energy to take the obvious first step, even when we have great contacts. Pinning down what gets in the way (fear of rejection, poor self-image, a need for certainty and concrete outcomes) is the job of the creative career coach, who needs to be a mix of magician and touchline encourager. So the real work isn't focused on activity at all, but what prevents it. What gets in the way of that first phone call? Interestingly, the steps to success are often baby steps – very often all that's required is to ask a friend or colleague for one piece of information.

The real art is helping clients to set goals *without getting in the way of them*. We are all gifted at blocking our own best ideas; it's too easy to find an inner negative voice. Change makes us more vulnerable than usual to fear of rejection or ridicule.

HEATHER GROSSMAN – DIRECTOR OF ASSETS AND RESOURCES FOR STOKE ON TRENT & STAFFS FIRE AND RESCUE SERVICE.

Heather had been Finance Director of a £50m turnover public sector organization for 12 years and was *'overdue for a change'*. At her first session Heather displayed a dissatisfaction with the 'same old' choices being offered her by the marketplace.

Heather strongly wanted to make the transition into a broader role: *'I knew I would have difficulty finding the right role because employers like to recruit people who have done the role somewhere else whereas I was looking for something new.'*

'John asked me to describe my perfect role, where I would be working, who I would be working with, what I would be doing, and helped me build up a checklist which I could measure opportunities by.'

Heather switched from a policy of unsuccessfully applying for a wide range of roles to targeting specific organizations and asking immediately to what extent the organization would welcome someone from outside the sector.

The Fire Service role was particularly attractive to Heather because her father had been a fire fighter. She was impressed with Staffordshire's record on community safety, performance, and cost reduction, and also felt that the planned PFI programme for fire stations matched her experience of property development.

Heather steeled herself for an interview. As a person with no fire service experience she expected to fall at the first hurdle: *'John explained that "being myself" was the most important thing at interview, and that the key to being successful was preparation, and then more preparation. The*

> *result? I now have a role which fascinates me every minute of every day, and gives me the opportunity to work with some great people. You can't ask for more than that, can you?'*

I often ask clients to define what would be the best and the worst outcome. The best is usually modest (an enjoyable job that hits most of their career drivers), while the worst can be catastrophic. We give far more energy to the dark picture – the one that will whisper to you at 2 o'clock in the morning 'You'll never get a job ...' There are external factors (the economy, location, industry decline) and real constraints (age, health, qualifications), but none are as powerful as the individual's mindset.

Clients are most responsive in the opening stages, when they are reflecting on who they are, and self-absorption provides a fascination high. The critical stage is to get clients to begin looking outwards to find out what the world of work has to offer. Career coaching is goal-oriented, and requires clients to manage their own futures. To do this, clients have to turn their attention outwards to real organizations and real jobs – a vital *research* step not to be confused with job search.

Strategies for helping clients who lack confidence to make an uncomfortable career change:

■ **Flagging the issue up at the beginning of the process**: *'By session 4 you might be saying to me ...'.*

■ **Coaching clients from the outset to plan to deal with rejection**. It is, after all, the most common experience of job-seekers since you are likely to be rejected for far more jobs and interviews than accepted.

■ **Encouraging clients to set up a support group** – two people who will encourage new ideas, remind you of past successes, and encourage increased networking.

■ **Getting the client to come up with a reason to begin infor-mational interviews**. Once a client has spotted an area of work that looks interesting, then it's only a matter of time before paper and screen sources of information don't deliver enough. If the client prompts the idea of speaking to real people, it works.

■ **Finding quick wins**. If they start with people they know well enough to phone without a moment's hesitation, they can get some positive results. I get clients to commit to contacting three named people they already know and trust.

■ Probing **how a client would undertake this activity if they were doing it for someone else** – stepping out of their personal situation prompts a wide range of new ideas.

■ **Forming a strong link between a client's passions and their research**. If it's a field of work they really care about, they will find a way of discovering more.

■ **Build on synchronicity** – connections and opportunities will sometimes just happen. Encourage your client to push on doors that appear to be opening unassisted …

■ **Making connections directly for a client**. Setting up meetings with past clients, friendly employers, recruitment consultants …

What we love to do, of course, is to turn the world into easy choices. The nation's favourite is to play the real/ideal game: 'either I have a job I love OR I get a job that will pay the bills'. If you turn the world into black and white, grey becomes inconvenient, but practitioners will tell you that gradual career change is far more common than overnight transformation.

Useful Websites

Unless stated otherwise, these websites provide information about UK jobs and job search methods in Britain.

CAREERS ADVICE, DEVELOPMENT AND EXPLORATION

https://team-belbin.com
Online Belbin team role analysis. (A small fee is charged)

www.careers.lon.ac.uk/output/Page178.asp
University of London Virtual Careers Library

www.careers-scotland.org.uk
Career advice and support in Scotland

www.cv-library.co.uk
CV creating website

www.cvservices.net
CV advice and guidance. The site offers appraisal of CVs

www.hobsons.com
Jobs and careers guidance for school leavers and graduates

www.howtointerview.com
US-based site offering an interview question bank searchable by job functions

www.insidecareers.co.uk
Careers advice and graduate vacancies. The site is constructed in association with a number of professional bodies

www.i-resign.com/uk/home
Advice on how to leave your job and help with getting another includes useful links to other sites

www.JobHuntersBible.com
The website supporting *What Color Is Your Parachute?* – contains a wealth of useful information

www.manpower.co.uk
The site of the major employment agency – contains a lot of useful market information for jobseekers

www.prospects.ac.uk
Comprehensive facilities for graduates, but also contains online self-assessment facilities and details of hundreds of occupations

PSYCHOMETRIC TESTING AND ASSESSMENT CENTRES

www.psychometrics.co.uk
Psychometric testing

www.shldirect.com
Careers guidance, the site also contains practice questions for various assessment testing

www.morrisby.co.uk
Psychometric tests from Morrisby, which include practice tests and guidance

www.ase-solutions.co.uk
Psychometric tests from ASE Solutions. The site includes practice tests and familarization tests

www.get.hobsons.co.uk/advice/interview-selection-centre
Advice on preparing for assessment centres

CAREER BREAKS

www.thecareerbreaksite.com
Links to information on taking a career break

www.wanderlust.co.uk/trip-planners
Information on planning and taking a career break

COMPANY INFORMATION

www.applegate.co.uk
A UK business directory

www.bbc.co.uk
Information on business, finance and markets

www.carol.co.uk
Direct links to the financial pages of listed companies in Europe and the USA. Registration is required to access annual reports

www.companieshouse.co.uk
Details on all UK limited companies. Company accounts can be downloaded for a small fee

http://finance.google.co.uk/finance?ned=uk&hl=en&tab =ne
Business News and financial information from Google

www.guidestar.org.uk
A free public website providing a source of information on UK registered charities

http://news.ft.com
Business news from the *Financial Times*

www.kellys.co.uk
A UK and overseas company database searchable by company name or product/service

www.kompass.co.uk
Overseas and UK companies searchable by executive or company name. Charges may apply

www.londonstockexchange.com
Information on UK quoted companies

www.marketingfile.com
Company listings from over 100 different databases on a chargeable basis

www.ukbusinesspark.com
News items on UK companies and business sectors

www.zoominfo.com
Specialised search engine for researching people and companies

www.linkedin.com
Networking tool that enables you to link your networking contacts together

http://europe.vault.com
Information on careers, industries and employers

JOB HUNTING

www.alljobsuk.com
Job board portal, lists the major and specialist job board sites

www.charitypeople.co.uk
A recruitment site for the not-for-profit sector

www.clickajob.co.uk
UK job search engine covering a wide range of sectors

www.cwjobs.co.uk
IT job specialists

www.eteach.com
Jobs in teaching

www.exec-appointments.com
Senior executive jobs

www.executivesontheweb.com
Executive and management job board

www.fish4.co.uk/iad/jobs
UK jobs

www.gappweb.com
Accounting and finance job site

www.gisajob.com
Claims to be the UK's largest free jobs website

www.greendirectory.net/jobs
Jobs in the green sector

www.goldjobs.com
Lists jobs paying over £100,000 a year

www.hcareers.co.uk
Job board for the restaurant and hospitality industries

www.jimfinder.com
Manufacturing and engineering job board

www.justengineers.net
Engineering jobs

www.jobcentreplus.gov.uk
Job centres and vacancies

www.jobsgopublic.com
Public sector jobs

www.jobsin.co.uk
The website splits into industry specialisms

www.jobs.ac.uk
Academic jobs

www.jobsearch.co.uk
A search engine which gives access to advertisements and allows your CV to be posted for employers to review

www.jobsineducation.co.uk
A commercial site advertising jobs in the education sector

www.jobsite.co.uk
Gives access to advertisements and allows your CV to be posted for employers to review. Covers UK and Europe

www.milkround.com/s4/jobseekers
Milk round for graduate careers opportunities

www.monster.co.uk
Thousands of jobs in the UK and abroad. Includes career advice

www.museumjobs.com
Specialist jobsite for positions in museums, libraries, archives and galleries

www.planetrecruit.com
Access to job advertisements in a wide range of countries

www.reed.co.uk
UK jobs in a wide range of industry sectors. The site can send vacancies to your mobile phone

www.secsinthecity.co.uk
Secretarial, PA and admin jobs

www.toplanguagejobs.co.uk
Specialist language job portal

www.topjobs.co.uk
Professional, technical management and graduate vacancies

www.totaljobs.com
UK jobs in a wide range of occupation

www.workthing.com
Job board and career information

CAREERS EVENTS

www.onelifelive.co.uk
Yearly event providing information and guidance on a wide variety of career options including self employment, career breaks and retraining

www.forum3.co.uk
Recruitment event for the not-for-profit sector

OTHER WEBSITES OF INTEREST TO JOB SEEKERS

www.acas.org.uk
Advisory, Conciliation and Arbitration Service

www.equalityhumanrights.com/en/Pages/default.aspx
  Equality and Human Rights Commission

www.emplaw.co.uk
  Provides information about employment law and gives
  access to law reports, etc.

www.direct.gov.uk/en/Employment/Employees/index.htm
  Government website containing information and guidance
  on a wide variety of employment matters

www.direct.gov.uk/en/index.htm
  The main site giving access to all government departments
  including the Department for Education and Skills

PROFESSIONAL ASSOCIATIONS

www.accountingweb.com
  A resource for the accounting profession

www.agcas.org.uk
  Association of Graduate Careers and Advice Services

www.agr.org.uk
  Association of Graduate Recruiters, i.e. employers who
  regularly recruit from universities

www.charitiesdirect.com
  A site listing all major charities and associations. Links to a
  jobs bank containing vacancies in the charity sector

www.cbi.org.uk
  Confederation of British Industry

www.cipd.co.uk
  Chartered Institute of Personnel and Development

www.cim.co.uk
  Chartered Institute of Marketing

www.engc.org.uk
  Engineering Council

www.hcima.org.uk
  Hotel and Catering International Management Association

www.interimmanagement.uk.com/pages/home.aspx
Interim Management Association

www.iod.com
Institute of Directors

www.iolt.org.uk
Institute of Logistics and Transport

www.managers.org.uk
Chartered Management Institute

www.mca.org.uk/mca
Management Consultancies Association

www.lawsoc.org.uk
The Law Society

www.rec.uk.com/home
The Recruitment and Employment Confederation's website with listings of employment agencies by region and specialism

HELP FOR DISABLED JOBSEEKERS

www.disability.gov.uk
The government's site on disability issues

www.radar.org.uk
A national organization that provides advice and support for the disabled.

www.skill.org.uk
Help for disabled students

NEWSPAPERS

www.jobs.telegraph.co.uk
The Daily Telegraph job sections.

http://bubl.ac.uk/link/n/newspapers.htm
Lists all UK main newspapers

www.careers.scotsman.com
  The Scotsman

www.fish4jobs.co.uk
  Covers a range of regional newspapers

http://news.ft.com/home/uk
  Financial Times

www.irishtimesjobs.com
  Irish Times

www.mediauk.com
  Media directory for the UK

www.timesonline.co.uk
  The Times

www.scottishnewspapers.com
  Lists Scottish newspapers

www.unison.ie/allpapers.php3
  Links to regional Irish newspapers

www.loadzajobs.ie
  Irish Independent

http://jobs.guardian.co.uk
  The Guardian job board

TRAINING AND COURSES

www.crac.org.uk
  Lifelong career development

www.homestudy.org.uk
  Association of British Correspondence Colleges

www.hero.ac.uk
  The official gateway site to the UK's universities, colleges
  and research organizations

www.learndirect.co.uk
  Information and advice on courses

www.niace.org.uk
National Association for Adult Continuing Education

www.jobcentreplus.gov.uk/JCP/Customers/New_Deal/ index.html
Information about the various New Deal schemes

www.open.ac.uk
Open University

www.ucas.ac.uk
University courses

CREATIVITY WEBSITES

www.bemorecreative.com
Helps build on your creative brain

www.mensa.org.uk/mensa/puzzles.html
IQ testing and Mensa puzzles

www.hbdi-uk.com
Details of the Herrmann Brain Dominance Instrument

www.ideasfactory.com
Practical information for careers in the creative field

Index